ASIAN RELIGIONS--HISTORY OF RELIGION:  1974 PROCEEDINGS

PREPRINTED PAPERS

FOR THE SECTION ON ASIAN RELIGIONS--HISTORY OF RELIGION

Compiled by

Harry Partin

AMERICAN ACADEMY OF RELIGION

ANNUAL MEETING

1974

Additional copies of this volume may be ordered from

Scholars' Press
Department of Religious Studies
University of Montana
Missoula, Montana  59801



ISBN  0-88420-114-7
Library of Congress Card Number:  74-14213

Published by
American Academy of Religion
Florida State University
Tallahassee, Florida
32306

TABLE OF CONTENTS

ORTHODOXY IN THE TAOIST TRADITION
Michael Saso
University of Hawaii

The term orthodoxy (Cheng 正 ) is commonly used among Taoists in a sense which is perhaps difficult for the outsider to understand, especially in the context of present day Chinese studies where emphasis has been placed on the Confucian and Buddhist traditions.  To many scholars, western and oriental alike, Taoism is at best sectarian, if not downright heterodox.  I would therefore like, in the present paper, to define the meaning of the word orthodoxy in the Taoist tradition. The sources for my discourse are twofold, namely, Taoists of Taiwan who consider themselves to be orthodox, and the Taoist Canon as a means to verify the authenticity of information gathered during field research. In the very beginning, I would like to lay to rest a difficulty put to me by my colleagues who object to the use of materials gathered from Taiwan as applicable to the rest of China.  It has been suggested to me, for instance, that studying Taoism in Taiwan is like going to Hawaii to understand typical American customs. My rejoinder to such a problem is to point to the obvious similarity between the Catholic Mass, and orthodox Taoist ritual; that is, one can go almost anywhere in the world and witness the same Mass being celebrated, whether in Spain, France, or Hawaii. So, too, one should be able to see authentic Taoist ritual wherever an orthodox Taoist is performing, providing that the ritual is literate, passed down from classical antiquity, and found in a published, standardized canon. It is the purpose of this paper to show that orthodoxy in the Taoist tradition depends  upon these three criteria, that is, orthodoxy for the Taoist depends up literacy, classical tradition, and canonicity, qualities which can be tested wherever a Taoist is to be found.

The words orthodoxy and heterodoxy are commonly used in English to translate the Chinese characters Cheng (正 ) and Hsieh (邪 ). The word Cheng is taken to mean "upright, true, orthodox, correct, regular, authorized," and so forth.  Its contrary Hsieh is taken to mean "heterodox, depraved, vicious, evil, harmful emanations, demonic magic," and so forth. Frequently the term Hsieh is simply used as a term of opprobrium for a person or a doctrine of a different persuasion than one's own. Thus the most sectarian of secret societies in China often speaks of the doctrines of a rival society as Hsieh, meaning lewd, misleading, liable to official persecution by the mandarin. To the Confucian literatus, both Buddhism and Taoism are often considered to be heterodox; but to the renewed gratitude of Buddhist and Taoist sects, the emperors of China did not always agree with the views of the lettered class, and patronized first one, then the other of the two great religious movements. The point in question, however, is not what the lettered official thought of the Taoist tradition, but rather what the Taoists themselves considered to be authorized and approved as orthodox for themselves. Thus, the opposite of orthodox in the Taoist sense need not be the heterodox, but rather the kind or style of liturgy which was not literate, classical, or cannical,  that is oral, popular, and local in origin.  Thus the distinction, in the Taoist sense, came to be made between the orthodox and the popular, the literate and the folk, the "black" and the "red" as is so charmingly said of the two genre by the devout faithful who patronize Taoist ritual in Taiwan.

The distinction between the orthodox and the popular, therefore, is not a fiction of the scholarly mind, but a difference noted by the pious faithful of Taiwan who frequent the temples and patronize the liturgical

services offered by the Taoist priests. There are in fact two kinds of Taoists in Taiwan, those who belong to the lettered, canonical, classical tradition, and those who practise a more popular, dramatic, and indigenous form of
rites. The former are called "Blackhead" and the latter "Redhead" Taoists in
common terminology. To the stately, orthodox Blackhead are relegated the
duties of burying the dead, because burial ritual makes use of the canonical
Yellow Register Fasts (Huang-lu Chai 黃籙齋). To the Redhead fall the duty
of exorcising the baleful, curing the sick, and interpreting the mumbling of
the possessed mediums. Due to the nature of the ministry, they are also known
as Hoat-ah (法仔) or "little magicians" in colloquial Taiwanese. Since Taoism is a confraternity of men and women drawn together by common interests,
the two groups often learn from one another. It is not uncommon that the
Blackheads participate in the rites of the Hoat-ah magicians, and the Redheads learn to imitate the splendid Gold Register ritual of renewal (金籙醮)
used in the lucrative village festival liturgies. But a Redhead is never
allowed to bury the dead, and a Blackhead does not act as an interpreter of
a possessed medium, functions which basically distinguish the two groups.

The traits which fundamentally distinguish the orthodox from the
popular Taoist are the following:

1. A literate, refined, stately tradition.
2. Doctrinal content truly descending from antiquity.
3. Revealed texts contained in an officially approved canon.

By the same token, the converse of these qualities  define the popular
Taoists and set them apart from their orthodox brethren:

1. Popular dramatic ritual in seven character doggerel verse.
2. Rituals from local or non-Chinese sources.
3. Texts which imitate the Canon, but are different in content.

In the following paragraphs I shall attempt to outline each of the above
characteristics in order to show that the orthodox tradition does indeed
exist in Taiwan, and that it is easily identifiable wherever Taoists are
functioning. That is to say, the principles outlined here can be applied to
Taoists amywhere in Asia, or where a traditional Chinese community is to be
found with Taoists in residence.

The first criterion of orthodoxy is literacy. Literacy is of two sorts,
the training of the Taoist himself who practises the rites, and the content of
the rites used in public and private liturgy.  Both qualifications are true
of the orthodox tradition, that is, orthodox Taoism is found among the lettered classes, and its content is literary in nature, requiring a man of learning to qualify for membership. In my experience of orthodox Taoism in north
Taiwan, orthodox Taoist masters have fulfilled both conditions, that is to
say, the five main clans of Hsinchu city now practising Taoism  in the orthodox tradition come from the official lettered class. The famous Lin family
of Hsinchu city, who founded the Cheng-i Tz'u-t'an confraternity for the
practise of orthodox Taoist ritual, provided the military officials for north
Taiwan during the ethnic wars of the late Ch'ing period. The four main members
of the confraternity from its inception in 1886, the Ch'en, Wu, Huang, and
Chuang clans, each had members who served as city officials during the Ch'ing,
the Japanese, and the Nationalist eras. Though only the poorer members of
the families actually practise ritual in the public forum in order to make a
living, all of the members still perform the meditations of internal alchemy,
and practise forms of breath control and macrobiotics. Classical Taoist ritual
is performed at an annual meeting of the members, which requires a knowledge

of classical Chinese, the T'ang-wen (唐文) or classical pronunciation, the
penmanship of a literatus, and the ability to compose classical essays and
ritual documents modeled after the format for imperial memorials, rescripts,
and so forth. The rituals of orthodox Taoism are therefore written in classical style, and require men of letters to perform properly. Though the members
of the clan who actually perform ritual for a living are the poorer branches
of a Taoist family, the leading Taoist masters belong to literatus-official
class of society.

The second criterion for orthodoxy in the Taoist tradition is the
possession of and ability to use ritual manuals which have been passed down
from antiquity.  There are three sets of ancient registers or styles of meditative liturgy which have been passed down from antiquity, the Meng-wei registers (盟威), the Ling-pao registers (靈宝), and the Shang-ch'ing
scriptures (上清). The first of these, the Meng-wei registers are said to
derive from Han Chung and the ritual of the first Heavenly Master, Chang Tao-
ling.[2] The second style of liturgy, typified by the Su-ch'i (宿啟) ritual
which is a part of every orthodox Taoist's repertoire but unknown to the
popular Redhead tradition, makes use of the Ling-pao Five Talismans (靈宝五符)
in a ritual which dates back to at least the 4th and 5th centuries of our
era, with the signature of the Taoist master Lu Hsiu-ching (d. 471 A.D.)[3] The
last mentioned Shang-ch'ing tradition is typified by the meditative rituals
of the Yellow Court Canon (Huang-t'ing Ching 黄庭経).[4] Taoists have been
graded at least since the T'ang dynasty according to their knowledge of the
classical registers, in a system which imitates the nine grades of the imperial mandarin (九品至一品) of the North-south period.  The possession and
mastery of the Yellow Court Canon, the meditative rituals of which require
a life of leisure and affluence in order to emulate, gives the highest Grade
One ordination. The fewer the manuals and the lesser the ability of the Taoist to perform the meditations and techniques of internal alchemy, the lower
the grade of ordination. Thus Taoists who depend for a livelihood on a simple
performance of ritual without the complicated ascesis of meditation and
macrobiotics are given the lower grades of ordination.

The third criterion for orthodoxy is canonicity. Ritual manuals
used by Taoists who claim orthodoxy must be the same in content as those
contained in the Taoist Canon. It was to the same Lu Hsiu-ching mentioned in
the above paragraph that the formation of the first Canon is usually attributed. Lu Hsiu-ching is said to have formulated the Canon into Three Arcana
(San-tung 三洞), based on the Shang-ch'ing revelations from Mao Shan, the
Ling-pao scriptures  and the Meng-wei registers mentioned above.[5] Besides
these ancient registers two others have been accepted as canonical, that is,
the Pole Star registers of Wu-tang mountain in Hupei, and the Ch'ing-wei (清微)
or Five Thunder magic registers from Hua Shan in Shensi. I have personally
tested the authenticity of the claims of the orthodox Taoists of Taiwan by
bringing copies of the Taoist Canon to Chiao  festivals (gold register) of
renewal and Chai services (yellow register) of burial. The texts of such
rites as the Su-ch'i (宿啟), Morning Audience (早朝), Noon Audience (午朝),
Night Audience (晚朝), and the other basic Chiao and Chai liturgies were
identical, that is, the orthodox Taoists of Taiwan could use their own manuscript volumes interchangeably with the canonical versions.[6] The Taiwan versions
were in fact more accurate, with fewer copyist errors, and the rubrics preserved in a systematic manner. The traditions of Taoist orthodoxy preserved in
Taiwan are, indeed an indispensable research aid for the study of religious
Taoism in the orthodox tradition. A set of the orthodox materials has recently been published by the Ch'eng-wen Press in Taipei, under the title Chuang-

Lin Hsü Tao-tsang (莊林續道藏) the titles from which I shall quote in the
appendix as an illustration of canonical materials which can be found in the
Canon published during the Cheng-t'ung reign years in the Ming dynasty.[7] The
Ch'eng-wen Press edition contains 50 manuals of gold register _Chiao_ rituals,
20 manuals of yellow register _Chai_ services, and 10 manuals of esoteric rubrics used in the performance of ritual in the orthodox style. The last section
of the collection contains 24 manuals of Redhead popular materials of which
articles 18-23 bear titles similar to the rituals of the orthodox canonical
tradition. By comparing such rituals as the morning audience, noon audience,
and night audience, the Redhead versions appear similar in name only with
the canonical texts, that is, the Redhead _Chiao_ is properly termed a "ministry of imitation" of the classical canonical liturgies.

The identifying features of popular ritual, seen in the liturgies of the Redhead
Taoists, therefore, do not fulfill the criteria for orthodoxy found in the
rites of the Blackhead Taoists.  Rites such as "opening the eyes" of a new
statue, that is, bringing the spirit of which the statue is a representation
inside the statue, is an imitation of a popular Buddhist rite brought from
popular Indian religion into China with Buddhism. Of the same genre is the
much talked-of dramatic sequence called "climbing the 36 sword ladder," a
Brahmin rite seen in such widely spread provinces as Orissa, the Punjab, and
the bordering states along the old silk route into China. The Redheads use
the sword ladder act as a sort of rite of initiation, imitating the possessed
mediums who prove their spiritual powers by imperviousness to pain or inci-
sion. The rite is often imitated by Blackhead Taoists anxious to compete in
the public market, just as the Redheads copy the stately liturgy of the _Chiao_.
The contents of the Redhead section of the _Chuang-lin Hsü Tao-tsang_ show in
fact a preponderance of seven character doggerel verse rather than literary
style in the composition of liturgical texts. The contents of the rituals
are popular, even foreign in nature, and the texts themselves are not canonical, even if the names sometimes bear similarities. The popular nature of
Redhead liturgy in no way is considered inferior to the stately orthodox rites
of the Blackheads, however; the Redhead rites are far more appealing to the
public, easier to follow and understand, and quite in demand during public
festivals, as well as daily services conducted in private houses and temples.

Thus there are many dramatic and colorful Redhead rites which are
to be seen almost daily in Taiwanese households, on the occasion of blessing
a new room or a new house, or exorcising a sickman of an evil spirit. In such
a ritual the Taoist enters the room of the sick man, or the room to be blessed,
and begins by mixing blood drawn from a cock's comb with blood taken from his
own tongue. The mixture is used by the Taoist as an ink with which to draw a
set of five talismans on yellow paper, which are hung on the walls as good
luck charms.  The Taoist then performs the rite a second time, using blood
drawn from a duck's bill. A reed mat is rolled up, and the two ends dipped in
kerosene.  With the ends afire, the Taoist twirls the mat around his head, and
strikes at spectres and demons hidden in the corners, in closets, and under
the sick person's bed.  Finally, a broom is taken in which a string of firecrackers have been hidden. The Taoist touches a stick of burning incense to
the wick, and sweeps out the room while the firecrackers are exploding. An
assistant awaits outside the door, to imprison the escaping demons in a
cloth sack. Another assistant waits on a motorbike to whisk the imprisoned
evil spirits away to the nearest stream. There, the bag of imprisoned evil
is thrown into the water, to be carried back to the realms of darkness in the
underworld. Such rites are a far cry from the stately classical rites of the
orthodox tradition, and immediately identifiable by their popular, dramatic

style of performance. The habit of the believers in Chinese religion who
frequent the temples and patronize Taoist ritual, of calling the two styles
"Red" and "Black" is therefore  understandable.  The Redhead Taoist is popular, local, uncanonical in nature. The Blackhead Taoist  uses a literate,
classical, canonical liturgy. In order to compete on the public market, the
two sometimes imitate each other, but a closer look at the content of the
two kinds of rituals shows them to be substantially different.

        The criteria for orthodoxy in the Taoist tradition are therefore
objectively verifiable. Wherever orthodox Taoists perform, the literate,
classical, canonical tradition of liturgical performance can be seen and
studied.  In as much as there are orthodox Taoists on Taiwan who use canonical texts, or in as much as there are orthodox Taoists in the diaspora of
Southeast Asia among the traditional Chinese communities, Taoism can be
usefully and profitably studied in its traditional classical form. The three
criteria listed above, that is, literate style, classical tradition descending from antiquity, and texts taken from the printed canon, can be used by
the field worker to identify orthodox Taoism  wherever a Chinese community
with a Taoist in residence is to be found.

## FOOTNOTES

1. _Hsinchu County Gazette_, Hsinchu Wen-hsien Wei-yüan Hui, Hsinchu, 1955.
   pp. 9-10.

2. _Han-chung_ (漢中) was the term given to that area of Szechuan where the
   Heavenly Master sect was founded. The _Fa Lu_ (發炉) and other typical rites
   of the method are described by the early 6th century master T'ao Hung-
   ching in the _Teng-chen Yin-chüeh_ to be found in volume 193 of the Canon.

3. The _Su-ch'i_ ritual with the signature of Lu Hsiu-ching and other early
   Taoists is to be found among other places in Vol. 281 of the Canon, Ch. 16.

4. The Shang-ch'ing tradition  dates from the three visionaries Yang Hsi,
   Hsü Yü, and Hsü Mi who received the _Yellow Court Canon_ and other manuals
   atop Mao Shan near Nanking at the end of the 4th century, during a series
   of nocturnal visions. Cf. Taoist Canon, _Chen Kao_, volumes 637-640.

5. Cf. Ch'en Kuo-fu, _Tao-tsang Yüan Liu K'ao._ Chung-hua press, Shanghai, 1949.

6. For a description of the content of these rituals, cf. my _Taoism and the
   Rite of Cosmic Renewal_, Washington State University Press, Pullman, 1972.

7. The _Chuang-lin Hsü Tao-tsang_, Ch'eng-wen Press, Taipei, 1974, 25 volumes,
   is divided into 4 sections, containing 103 Chuan  from the family libraries
   of the _Cheng-i Tz'u-t'an_ members in Hsinchu city. The 50 manuals in the
   Gold Register _Chiao_ section (part I) can be compared with the _Wei-i_ or
   liturgical part of the _Tung-hsüan Pu_, Part Two of the Canon.

金籙　五朝醮事　盟威經籙道士傳用

1. 百神燈（光緒發未年梅月法應壇翁清潭抄）法廳壇記

2. 發表　發奏燈齋科儀　通靈壇　甲午季冬月重抄

3. 開光科儀（光緒拾年歲次甲申花月吉旦）法應壇翁記

4. 請神　祝聖科儀（光緒甲申拾年蒲月）法元壇翁清潭抄

5. 禁壇（光緒戊子年花月蘊輝氏吉置）

6. 玉樞經（印）

7. 午供　九陳供科（光緒玖年歲次癸未納月）法應壇抄錄法應壇記

8. 午供（光緒癸未年花月）通靈壇　陳森員抄

9. 午供　法應壇記

10. 朝天卷一（道光貳拾伍年歲次乙巳桐月吳周巖抄立）

11. 朝天卷二（同上　　　　　桐月　　　　　）

12. 朝天卷三（同上　　　　　梅月　　　　　）

13. 朝天卷四（同上　　　　　梅月　　　　　）

14. 朝天卷五（同上　　　　　梅月　　　　　）

15. 朝天卷六（同上　　　　　梅月　　　　　）

16. 朝天卷七（同上　　　　　蒲月　　　　　）

17. 朝天卷八（同上　　　　　蒲月　　　　　）

18. 朝天卷九（同上　　　　　瓜月　　　　　）

19. 朝天卷十（同上　　　　　瓜月　　　　　）

20. 宿啓　太上金籙宿啓科範　法應壇抄玄應壇陳丁鳳記

21. 重白　平氣卷　正一嗣壇　林元悟記　六十一代天師門下

22. 早朝（大清光緒拾年孟夏月）源應壇黃法抄置

　　分燈科儀　法廳壇記

24. 捲簾　法廳壇記

25. 振鐘磬（大清光緒癸未年荔月）法應壇翁清潭抄

26. 三官經（大清光緒拾壹年歲次乙酉瓜月吉旦）源應壇黃法盥手重抄

27. 三官經（印）

28. 三官寶懺　天卷（光緒拾捌年歲次壬辰陽月穀旦）法應壇翁清潭抄

29. 三官寶懺　地卷（同上）

30. 三官寶懺　人卷（同上）

31. 午朝（大清光緒拾年歲次甲申孟夏元月）源應壇黃法重抄

32. 東斗經（光緒癸未年桐月吉日翁清源抄）

33. 西斗經（同上）

34. 南斗經（道光甲午年瑞月念日許榮撮）

35. 北斗經（咸豐丁巳年中冬）江西南城信士吳蘭芳谷氏重敬刊

36. 中斗經（光緒癸未年桐月吉日）翁清潭抄　法應壇記

37. 玉皇經日卷（印）

38. 玉皇經月卷（印）

39. 玉皇經星卷（印）

40. 玉皇懺科（咸豐玖年歲己未蒲月朔日）法眞壇吳周巖抄置

41. 晚朝（大清光緒拾年孟夏六月）源應壇黃法抄立

42. 登臺（光緒玖年歲次癸未納月日）法應壇抄錄

43. 九幽懺　一～二卷（印）

44. 九幽懺　三～四卷

45. 九幽懺　五～六卷

46. 九幽懺　七～八卷

47. 九幽懺　九～十卷

48. 道場（正醮）（光緒癸未年桐月）法應壇翁清潭抄

49. 道場副本初卷秘訣

50. 普度登臺說法　二卷（昭和癸酉年十二月六日抄）

### Section 2.　Burial Ritual

黃籙　午夜喪事　玉府烏頭道士專用

1. 靈寶拔亡發表儀（通靈壇民國癸卯年四月初八日莊陳登雲敬抄）天上五星二
   十八宿地中五方水裏十州山萬神發表黃籙喪事

2. 玉府祝聖（即請神）科儀（通靈壇民國癸卯年四月初九日通靈壇莊陳登雲敬
   抄）

3. 靈寶度人經上部（於正統道藏度人經同）

4. 靈寶洞玄無量度人經中部（民國五十五年農曆五月初十戊午日通靈壇陳登雲
   敬抄）

5. 靈寶度人經（下部）

6. 太乙慈悲道場三元滅罪水懺法卷

7. 玉府頒赦科儀（民國五十五年歲次丙午五月初四日通靈壇　登雲敬抄）

8. 靈寶煉度宗旨全集（通靈壇）（後天八卦超度亡魂早超昇）

9. （同上）煉度宗旨（通靈壇陳捷記）

19. 靈寶拔度藥師寶懺（通靈壇 光緒庚寅年梅月 陳捷記）

20. 沐浴（於十一號同）召魂沐浴給牒科

文檢　符咒秘訣 Section Three. Rubrics.

1. 吳氏文檢

2. 醮喪式三五朝文檢通靈壇記　捷三

3. 正一嗣壇師傳符咒訣（不全）

4. 劉氏文檢

5. 文檢辛卯季春法眞壇抄（道光貳拾壹年桐月季春法眞壇吳景春抄）

6. 意文符咒

7. 茅山呪語

8. 同長樂軒　希文氏

9. 設醮道場登臺拜表玉訣科儀

10. 金籙早午晚朝遣將召四靈科儀（通靈壇）

閭山神霄小法　紅頭神霄法師傳用　　Section Four. Redhead Rites.

1. 夫人科（通靈陳記）

2. 起土開金井刈閭科儀（辛申年新源重抄）與十七卷同

3. 請夫人科（法應壇）

4. 唐山科儀童限下帝付送神三元科儀（道光貳拾陸年歲次丙午蒲月）與周巖重抄

5. 解連妙經（通靈壇）

6. 閭山秘訣

7. 吾有社稷眞官神咒當持誦

8. 依錢造橋科儀

9. 申文科（功德發表科儀）（通靈壇陳記）（歲次丙午年五月吉且眾利玉記）

10. 賞軍科儀（歲次在道光乙亥午靈月朔日）新社壇記

11. 新刻元龜會解斷易神書卷下（林永記）

12. 申牡科（道光貳拾陸年歲次丙午閏五月吉且）法眞壇吳周巖抄

13. 造錢一段（造錢科）

14. 關聖帝君明聖眞經（序括小法秘咒）（光緒甲午重鐫）

15. 拜斗科（修眞壇記）

16. 解連妙經（眾等壽元賽過彭祖）

17. 起土開金井刈閭科儀八房科

18. 靈寶大正臺發表眞科　神霄醮用科儀劉氏傳

19. 靈寶正臺清晨啓請玄科（請神）

20. 靈寶早朝科儀

21. 靈寶正臺午朝科儀

22. 靈寶正臺晚朝科儀

23. 二十三太上靈寶正臺宿朝玄科

24. 送般科儀

# NEO-CONFUCIANISM, SAGEHOOD AND THE RELIGIOUS DIMENSION

Rodney L. Taylor
University of Virginia

The figure of the sage (sheng/sheng jen)[a] has occupied a position of paramount importance in the Confucian tradition. Such sages in classical Confucianism were culture heroes and kings, each a paradigm of virtue and model for emulation. There is a sense, however, in which these sages were remote and distant; most were far removed in time. The virtues of such sages also seem strangely removed from the capabilities of the vast majority of persons. Mencius can express the optimistic stance that anyone is capable of becoming a Yao[b] or Shun[c],[1] but it seems far more accurate to describe this as an ideal rather than a practical goal of cultivation and learning.

As the Confucian tradition developed in new directions during the Sung[d] Dynasty (960-1279) a reinterpretation of the role of sagehood emerged. The concept of sagehood was removed from the past and became a realistically sought after goal attainable through a process of self-cultivation. A complex core of historical reasons have been discussed to account for this change and reorientation which saw the attainment of sagehood as the goal of the cultivation process.[2]

The new focus upon sagehood is expressed admirably in the Chin ssu lu[e] of Chu Hsi[f] (1130-1200) and Lü Tsu-ch'ien[g] (1137-1181).[3] The second chapter begins with the passage, "The sage aspires to become Heaven, the worthy aspires to become a sage and the gentleman aspires to become a worthy."[4] Sagehood is presented as something that can be cultivated and through proper cultivation is attainable. It is said that Chang Tsai[h] (1021-1077) told his students, "not to stop learning until they were equal to the sage."[5] Ch'eng I[i] (1033-1107) and Ch'eng Hao[j] (1032-1085) were both said to desire at an early age the learning necessary to become sages.[6] Though the effort and diligence required is not minimized, sagehood is strikingly presented as something attainable.

Our purpose here is to explore in some detail the nature of the goal of sagehood based primarily upon a study of the writings of the late Ming[k] Dynasty (1368-1644) Neo-Confucian Kao P'an-lang[l] (1562-1626).[7] The question raised is how best to understand sagehood and its cultivation. If sagehood can be characterized as a religious goal and self-cultivation as religious activity, on what grounds can the category religious be applied? Such a question has important ramifications for our understanding of Confucianism and the basis upon which it might be spoken of as a religious tradition. If we can get some sense of the structure and definition of the religious dimension within the Confucian tradition, an adequate, if not sound, approach to the position of the religious dimension within the Chinese tradition as a whole might be one step closer.

<u>On the Nature of Sagehood</u>
For the Neo-Confucian masters of the Sung Dynasty sagehood became an achievable goal possible through the correct cultivation.

The _Chin ssu lu_ is an excellent example of a manual whose teachings
were directed towards the cultivation and eventual realization of
sagehood.  It is of some significance in this context to understand
clearly what was meant by sagehood and how the state of sagehood was
characterized.[8]

Sagehood is characterized in numerous ways reflecting in
large part differences between individual Neo-Confucians.  There
exists, however, a broad area of agreement on several of the major
features.  Sagehood may well be considered as a particular way of
looking at the world.  Often expressed is a feeling of harmony or a
sense of oneness with all things.  The _Chin ssu lu_ records, for
example, a statement by Chang Tsai, "By enlarging one's mind, one can
enter into all things in the world.  As long as anything is not yet
entered into, there is still something outside the mind."[9]  Chang Tsai
regards as central to the definition of the sage a feeling of unity
between self and others.  Ch'eng Hao through his expression that, "The
man of jen[m] forms one body with all things without any differentiation,"[10] clearly indicates the import of a unitary view to the content
of sagehood.  The _Chin ssu lu_ is explicit in directing discipline and
effort towards a point where self and others may be spoken of as form-
ing a unity.  "Combine the internal and the external into one and
regard things and the self as equal.  This is the way to see the fundamental point of the Way."[11]  Inherent in the characterization of sagehood is this quality of "unity," i.e. seeing oneself and others as in
some sense equal.

The question arises as to precisely what is meant in speaking of a unity and in what sense self and others can be regarded as
the same.  The sage is he who has fully realized his own nature or
hsing[n].  He is aware of the Principle, li[o], within himself and all
things.  What seems to unite the sage with all things is the understanding of a uniform Principle, ethical in form within self and all
else.  Chang Tsai's "Western Inscription" eloquently testifies to the
sense of unity, a unity grounded in a common ethical structure.[12]  All
men are united through their common natures of _jen_, humanity.  They
are united not only with each other, but with Heaven and earth and all
things.  Ch'eng Hao in his essay dealing with the nature of _jen_ cites
Chang Tsai's "Western Inscription" as an illustration of the uniformity
of man's ethical nature in all things.[13]  Ch'eng Hao's understanding
of Chang Tsai is expressive of the foundation for a unitary view.

The unity or oneness expressed is an "identity" of self and
others through a common structure found in all things.  The Principle,
_li_, of one's nature is the Principle, _li_, of the nature of Heaven and
earth.  It does not seem to be the case that self and others are
"identical" as a category of "being" or "substance," rather that the
unity is established through Principle, _li_, understood as the ethical
nature of _jen_ which is common to all things.  The Neo-Confucian employ-
ment of expressions of unity or oneness is to be understood as
referring to such an ethical structure.  The sage is he who in a very
real sense experiences this structure. Man's true nature, _hsing_, has
fully emerged in the sage.  Through the realization of this true
nature, the sage moves into a conscious rapport with Heaven, earth and
the myriad things.  Such rapport is possible because of the recognition
of  Principle, _li_, or Heavenly Principle, _T'ien li_[p], within all things.

## Sagehood, Neo-Orthodoxy and Kao P'an-lung

We have seen the emerging interest in devoting diligence and effort to the achievement of sagehood during the Sung period. Moving into the Ming Dynasty the abiding interest in the cultivation of sagehood continues and develops in new ways.

At issue throughout the Ming period was the manner in which the cultivation process should proceed. The school of Wang Yang-ming[q] (1472-1529) challenged the Ch'eng-Chu[r] understanding of self-cultivation. Ch'eng-Chu followers in turn questioned the validity of Wang Yang-ming's re-interpretation. deBary has suggested a very useful concept to account for much of the difference between Chu Hsi's emphasis upon broad learning and Wang Yang-ming's direct realization of sagehood through liang chih[s] or "innate knowing," what he calls the "burden of culture."[14] The Sung Dynasty passed on a legacy of voluminous accumulations of learning. The sheer quantity of material which, if one followed Chu Hsi, was to be investigated broadly, could become a toilsome if not burdensome responsibility. Wang Yang-ming reacted in part by shifting the center of study from broad learning to what he considered the primal source, the mind itself.

It is not, however, only Wang Yang-ming and his schools that felt such a burden. Indeed, the Ch'eng-Chu school of the Ming also redirected itself, placing less emphasis upon book learning.[15] This is a factor to consider in the Tung-lin[t] Academy and in particular in Kao P'an-lung. Allegiance is traced to Chu Hsi but not without certain modifications of interpretation.[16]

The ideal of sagehood becomes in a way even more dominant in Ming Neo-Confucianism than in the Sung masters, for Wang Yang-ming, through shunning dependency upon broad learning and by stressing interior realization, made the goal seem suddenly more accessible. The goal of sagehood had become relevant for the masters of the Sung. For those of exceptional talent and indefatigable effort, it was a practical goal. For the Neo-Confucians of the Ming, however, the ideal of sagehood was not only relevant, but also far more accessible.

One of the sources of tension between the various schools of Neo-Confucianism during the Ming was precisely this accessibility of the goal of sagehood. For Wang Ken[u] (1483-1540), founder of the T'ai-chou[v] School, sagehood was to be found in the common man. According to Wang Ken the true nature is to be seen in the most ordinary of tasks. Simple people going about their daily activities are the paradigms of sagely wisdom. For other members of the T'ai-chou School such as Yen Chün[w] and Lo Ju-fang[x] (1515-1588) sagehood was to be characterized by uninhibited and spontaneous behavior. deBary has emphasized the vitality of the T'ai-chou School and the revolutionary character of its message which brought sagehood to the level of the uneducated masses.[17] The vitality was not, however, something with which everyone had sympathy.

The Tung-lin Academy shared no enthusiasm for the T'ai-chou School. The Tung-lin represents what we might call a neo-orthodoxy. Neo-orthodoxy is understood to mean a reemergence of loyalty to the Ch'eng-Chu tradition, a strong expression of opposition to both Buddhism and the radical followers of Wang Yang-ming and an abiding

interest in rectifying government.  In order to establish a practical
guideline of definition I am viewing neo-orthodoxy as characteristic
of both the Tung-lin Academy (<u>Tung lin shu yüan</u>)[y] and what became
known as the Tung-lin party or faction (<u>Tung lin tang</u>)[z].[18]  The Tung-
lin Academy was an example of the general tendency in the Sung and
Ming dynasties to establish separate institutions of learning.[19]  The
Tung-lin party, as the name indicates, represented the political
influence and pressure exerted by men with Tung-lin sympathies.

        Instead of viewing the T'ai-chou School as a creative and
vital center bringing the cultivation of sagehood to the masses, the
Tung-lin looked upon such developments as largely responsible for a
breakdown in standards of behavior and morality.  Ku Hsien-ch'eng's[aa]
(1550-1612) attack on Li Chih[ab] (1527-1602) as a man who only affirms
what others deny is representative of the Tung-lin position.[20]  From
the Tung-lin point of view the radical followers of Wang Yang-ming did
not take seriously enough the problem of the cultivation of sagehood.
They made far too light a task of the learning process, ignoring the
lengthy effort and diligence required.  The Tung-lin was also virtually
unanimous in its opposition to Buddhism and particularly vehement
toward what they saw as Buddhist influences within Wang's followers.[21]
In addition to the neo-orthodox attitude towards the T'ai-chou School
and Buddhism, a grievous concern was exhibited over issues of corruption.  Huang Tsung-hsi[ac] (1610-1695) in his introductory remarks on
the Tung-lin School, directs his attention towards the efforts made in
routing out corruption that occupied much of the Tung-lin energies.[22]

        It is within this setting that we find Kao P'an-lung.  Kao
is a paradigm of the neo-orthodox movement for he opposed Wang Yang-
ming and his followers and was vehement in his opposition to Buddhism
even though he, like the Tung-lin School itself, may have also been
influenced, often in subtle ways, by both Wang Yang-ming and Buddhism.[23]
We do not want to lose sight of the fact, however, that central to this
neo-orthodox position is the ideal of sagehood.  Opposition might be
expressed towards Wang Yang-ming and others, but the opposition is
based upon what others say of the methods and processes necessary to
reach the goal rather than a criticism of the goal itself.  Sagehood
itself is maintained as the primary if not the only proper goal of the
learning process and is understood to be the realization of the true
nature, a nature of virtue which unites man with all things.

        For Kao P'an-lung too sagehood is the focus and aim of the
learning and cultivation process.  In his autobiography <u>K'un hsüeh
chi</u>[ad], "Recollection of the Toils of Learning," Kao asserted that it
was only at the age of twenty-five that he "resolved to pursue learning to become a sage."[24]  It cannot be said that Kao had been
indifferent to learning up to that point, for his own educational
foundation was well established.[25]  Instead, at this point Kao felt
that his learning had taken on a new character, a focusing on the goal
of sagehood as its aim.  It is a decisive change involving a fundamental reorientation of goals.  The unequivocal and uncompromising
nature of this change is indicated in Kao's writing.  He, "resolved to
pursue learning to become a sage," <u>chih yü hsüeh yi wei sheng jen</u>[ae].[26]
The emphasis is upon the "resolution," <u>chih</u>[af], that is involved.
Sagehood was dramatically seen as the culmination of the learning
process.  The act of the orientation to this goal is not to be minimized; it is the establishment of a legitimate goal, legitimate in the
sense of a meaningful and proper end of the learning process.  This

initial change Kao attributes to the discussions he heard between Li
Yüan-chung[ag], the District Magistrate of Wu-hsi[ah], and Ku Hsien-ch'eng,
eventually with Kao the co-founder of the Tung-lin Academy.[27]

Kao was already engaged in certain forms of self-cultivation
prior to the year 1586 in which he heard the discussions between Li and
Ku.[28]  He set up a strict schedule for himself, regulating his daily
affairs from morning till night and kept a diary of self-examination,
Jih chien pien[ai].[29]  Such activities might well be considered as forms
of self-cultivation and yet they are not included in the K'un hsüeh
chi as early stages in Kao's practices.  For Kao the record of self-
cultivation presented begins with this resolution to reach the goal of
sagehood.  In retrospect activities prior to that resolution, even if
they were forms of self-cultivation, lacked clear focus or aim.

Though the nature of the discussions Kao was witness to is
not touched upon, one thing about them is clear, they sparked the ideal
of sagehood within Kao.  Learning was no longer without direction, but
focused.  The relevance of this ideal is obvious in Kao's optimistic
stance, "There must be a way to become a sage."[30]  The goal had been
properly established and thus cultivation could begin.

## Sagehood and Soteriology

We have seen clearly the centrality of the goal of sagehood
for Kao P'an-lung.  Self-cultivation is pursued through constant
effort and diligent struggle.  On the basis of the ideal of sagehood
and the forms of self-cultivation undertaken to reach sagehood, the
question arises of the most accurate way to understand the goal itself.
Can we in some manner call this a religious goal?  If it is to be so
designated, then on precisely what grounds is it religious?

In a discussion of this kind the problem of the definition
of religion immediately arises.  For purposes of a general guideline
I have adopted Frederick Streng's definition of religion, "a means of
ultimate transformation."[31]  It is important also to take into account
Wach's four criteria of religious experience.[32]  The four criteria
though specifically describing religious experience, provide a useful
guide to distinguishing religious from non-religious experiences.[33]
As such they complement Streng's definition.  If a set of ideas or
practices conforms to Streng's explanation of religion as "ultimate
transformation" and matches the four criteria Wach employs to judge
religious experience, then the material being dealt with is to be
regarded as religious.

Streng considers as essential to his definition of religion
what he calls "ultimacy."[34]  Ultimacy is the "power and insight to
distinguish between what is real or true and what is secondary,
derivative, or even false."[35]  Ultimacy is thus knowing what is true
or authentic.  Such a sense of ultimacy permits one to live what
Streng calls an "authentic life."  A religious tradition within this
rubric of definition possesses a sense of ultimacy for it distinguishes
between what is true and what is false.  Thus it can propose a way of
living necessary to conform or become genuinely in accord with what
is viewed as true.  Such a way of living can be spoken of as the
"authentic life" for an individual in a particular tradition.  Wach's
first criterion of religious experience, "a response to what is

experienced as Ultimate Reality,"[36] further defines the character of
an "authentic life." It is the act of responding to something, rather
than an entirely subjective experience. The state of ultimacy and the
authentic life are not simply distinctions between what is true and
what is false, but a response to what is claimed to be true. It is
here that the element of transformation comes into play. To conform
to the "authentic life" is to be "transformed" from what is false to
what is true.

For Kao the sense of "true" must be seen within the context
of his own concerns. Central to these concerns is the attempt to
understand the hsing, true nature. Self-cultivation contributes
towards the understanding and expression of man's true nature while
sagehood represents the point at which the true nature may be said to
have reached unfoldment. If we attempt to define what "true" means
for Kao we need only return to the Ch'eng-Chu[37] presupposition that
all men possess a hsing which unites them not only with all other men,
but with Heaven and earth through the common ethical structure or
Principle, li. It is precisely this hsing that Kao regards as "true."
This understanding of hsing is suggestive of Streng's definition of
religion, possessing that which is considered ultimately true and
encouraging the movement or transformation from what is false to what
is true. If this is an accurate portrayal of the full dimension of
meaning within hsing, then we are not out of line to suggest a relation between hsing and religious structure. Hsing from this point of
view possesses the nature of the religious, and sagehood as the transformation into the full emergence of the hsing may be spoken of as a
religious goal. The sense in which sagehood is a transformation into
what is considered as true is suggestive of its soteriological
potentiality.

Self-cultivation is the means through which to understand,
to develop and to express the true nature. Through self-cultivation
the goal can be reached and thus self-cultivation may be said to
possess the power to bring to fruition the emergence of the true
nature.[38] Pursuing the goal of sagehood and acting in conformance
with the true nature, both may be considered as being "authentic" to
one's nature. Thus a life of self-cultivation might well be described
as an "authentic life." This is not altogether unlike Wach's fourth
criterion of religious experience, that there is an imperative to
issue in action.[39] Religious experience according to Wach is produc-
tive of practice. Self-cultivation could come under the rubric of
such practice or action for it is perhaps most accurately described as
a style of life. It is comprehensive and thorough and gives direction
to one's thoughts and actions.

Those thoughts and actions that form part of the self-
cultivation process as a style of life have inherent within them a
religious dimension. They share in the concern for what is considered
true, the true nature itself. This opens the possibility of seeing
the very concerns that have for so long seemed to differentiate
Confucian thought from a religious dimension as possessing the nature
of the religious. Civil service examinations, service in the government, or the fulfillment of responsibilities to family and community
appear as secular functions expressing humanistic concern, but devoid
of religious structure. Yet if such actions are seen as part of the

self-cultivation process they are no longer so simply and unequivocally
secular.  The direction is towards the unfoldment of the true nature
and self-cultivation is the style of life that is authentic, for its
goal is the expression of the true nature in sagehood.

To turn to the authentic life may mean the establishment of
a direction, of a goal in sight, but it does not end possible feelings
of anxiety on the part of the individual.  Kao's anxiety results from
his feelings of inadequate capacity when faced with the depth and
breadth of the goal and from his feeling of inadequate effort when
faced with the distance of the goal.  The K'un hsüeh chi concludes by
emphasizing the need to struggle on, to keep trying no matter how
miniscule progress may appear.[40]  There is a sense here both of complete involvement and intensity on the part of Kao.  Kao is responding
totally to what is viewed as ultimately true.  His whole being is
involved.[41]  In addition there are two senses of intensity for Kao.[42]
His diligent effort and his resolute struggle reveal an intensity of
pursuit after the true nature.  His breakthroughs to understanding
reveal the intensity of encounter with the true nature.

Inherent within our definition of religion is transformation, the movement from what is false to what is true.  There is for
Kao a sense of transformation as he moves from an aimless drifting
state to one with clear focus upon the goal of sagehood.  It is a
pivotal point in the K'un hsüeh chi when the goal of sagehood is first
focused upon.  It is the movement from what is false to what is true
or authentic.  The emergence of the true nature becomes the focus of
attention.  Within this focus are the seeds of religion.

A Sense of Transcendence
Sagehood and self-cultivation are not isolated phenomena.
There are contingent factors that enter into any consideration and
characterization of sagehood as a religious goal.  Several of these
are of interest to our inquiry for they represent forms of the
religious dimension not readily associated with the Confucian tradition.

The first such factor is what might be called a form of
transcendence.  This is of course a very difficult word to employ and
some degree of caution is warranted to avoid pitfalls such as Ninian
Smart has indicated.[43]

In suggesting the use of the word transcendence I have no
intention of alluding to a theological dichotomy between the world and
and that which is regarded as the Transcendent.  For Kao the salient
concern is the search for that which unites Heaven, earth and man
rather than that which differentiates them.  Heaven, earth and man all
possess Principle , li.  They may each have their proper sphere, but
they are not rigidly distinguished from each other in terms of a
distinct nature or essential structure.  A distinction between the
world and the Transcendent appears quite inoperative in this context.

Instead it might be suggested that the word transcendence
could be applied, though with some care, to a specific type of experience.  The experience would apply to particular moments along a
continuum of what could be described as the understanding of one's
true nature or hsing.  Such a continuum would extend from a point

characterized by the lack of any appreciable understanding to the
opposite end marked by the full realization of the Principle within
one's nature, i.e. sagehood.  Transcendence within this prescribed
continuum is a breakthrough into a new perspective or a greater understanding.  In such moments as they occur in Kao's writing he seems to
overcome the limitations of a former situation.  There is an emphasis
placed upon moving beyond such limitations.  This sense of moving
beyond ones present position, of gaining new insight within the process
of self-cultivation indicates the context of the use of transcendence.
It is important at this point to limit somewhat the perimeters for the
descriptive use of transcendence.  The context is essential.  It is
not at all certain that lacking the concerns of sagehood, references
described as experiences of transcendence could necessarily be considered as religious by virtue of such transcendence alone.  What
seems instead a significant factor for the religious import of the
experience of transcendence for Kao is the context within which such
experiences must be reckoned, i.e. the cultivation of sagehood.

This sense of transcendence is expressed in several of Kao's
writings.  The Shui chü chi[aj], "Recollections of the Water Dwelling,"[44]
concerns Kao's building of a small hermitage by the side of a lake to
pursue in a quiet and scenic spot his meditation and other forms of
self-cultivation.  In his discussion of his hermitage, the Water
Dwelling, an increasing level of transcendence is indicated.  After
time spent in the Water Dwelling Kao speaks of merging himself with
the progression of the seasons and the water itself.  "Dwelling here
at length, the owner, witnessing the risings and settings of sun and
moon, the formation and dispersion of cloud and mist, the flourishing
and perishing of trees and grasses, the comings and goings of animals
and fishes, merged in turn into the same water as the four seasons
and all things.  In it all he no longer thought of himself."[45]  Kao
seems to be expressing a certain understanding of the underlying unity
found in the various natural processes he had been witness to.  With
this awareness of unity there is a movement beyond self-conscious
concern.  After even longer spent in his hermitage Kao's sense of
unity broadens to encompass a larger sphere.  "Dwelling here even
longer, the owner, coming to rest in the vast silence of Heaven,
feasting upon the richness of the Primal Harmony,[46] straddling the
Flowing Forces[47] winging to and fro, ascended and descended through
the Gate of the Inexhaustible.[48]  In it all he no longer thought of
the water."[49]  Dwelling with the changing seasons the water is a
symbol of what is constant and what unifies.  Kao is no longer separated, he too can pass into the water for he has recognized the
common structure in himself and all things.  Yet after dwelling even
longer Kao moves beyond the symbol of the unifying element itself.
There is no implication of a state beyond the moral distinction of
good and bad.  Kao is saying only that he no longer depended upon the
water to convey the awareness of an underlying unity.  It is a significant statement though, for paradoxically he no longer needs the water
to see the unity of the water.  This is an expression of the experience of transcendence.

K'o lou chi[ak], "Recollections of the Suitable Loft,"[50] also
contains an element of transcendence.  The text describes a loft that
Kao built onto his Water Dwelling.  The loft is spoken of as k'o[al],
suitable, for it is that which is appropriate, according to Kao, for

the cultivation of sagehood.  Kao describes in great detail the merits
of the loft for his self-cultivation and states, "It is all that one
could want to while away the hours; suitable even to end one's days in.
Thus I named it 'Suitable Loft' which means it is suitable to my
aspirations."[51]  It is that which will facilitate the reaching of his
highest ideal, the realization of sagehood.  Kao found then that which
he considered "suitable" for his aspirations.  At the same time, however, there is the awareness that by making the decision to consider
the loft and its surroundings "suitable" other settings might well be
considered "unsuitable."

> "If all mountains and waters have a single purpose, then my
> presence in this loft is suitable.  If that is the case, then
> where there is that which is suitable, there is also that
> which is unsuitable.  We are still separate from things.  Ah!
> but if I could only forget about what is suitable and forget
> too what is unsuitable, the loft [called] suitable could be
> cast off."[52]

Living and thinking in categories of suitable and unsuitable we have
yet to sense the full dimension of unity between ourselves and things.
Alluding to Chuang Tzu, Kao laments that if he could only forget such
distinctions he would be freed from the loft itself.  There would be
nothing more suitable than anything else, no separation and no division in the fundamental unity of things.  This level of transcendence
is an ideal for Kao.  His initial task is to let the Suitable Loft
hold his aspirations, and proceed with the process of self-cultivation.

Further evidence of the element of transcendence is provided
in Kao's autobiographical writing the K'un hsüeh chi.  In a very personal and intimate style Kao speaks of the difficulties experienced
in the course of cultivation of sagehood.  The difficulties seem
extensive and in some cases insurmountable and yet there are moments
when a little understanding is gained.  Such moments move beyond the
limitations at hand and provide in a very concrete sense a breakthrough to further understanding.  Several examples from the K'un
hsüeh chi illustrate the manner in which these breakthroughs are
experienced.

In 1592 to correct what he saw as shortcomings in his own
cultivation, Kao adhered to a strict schedule of practices.  Lengthy
periods of "quiet-sitting," ching tso[am], resulted as Kao searched for
what he described to be the "original substance," pen t'i[an] of his
nature.[53]  One particular day he had been engaged in quiet-sitting for
an extended period when quite abruptly a breakthrough occurred.  Kao
says that he suddenly throught of the sentence from the I Ching[ao],
"He does away with what is false and preserves his integrity."[54]  Kao
records that there was an immediate realization of the import of the
statement.  He had not previously comprehended the relation between
"integrity," ch'eng[ap] and his own true nature.  In describing his new
found understanding Kao emphasizes the inherent relation between
ch'eng and hsing.  "I realized that in the immediate response (tang
hsia)[aq] 55 [of the nature] there was nothing false, for it possessed
integrity making it unnecessary to search after integrity."[56]  What
concerns us here is not the issue of the relation between ch'eng and
hsing in the immediate response or natural impulse, tang hsia, of the

nature,[57] but rather the manner in which Kao comes to understand this relation. Kao is describing a type of experience which provides him with at least a brief glimpse into further understanding of his nature. The way in which the experience is spoken of is significant to the issue of transcendence. Kao speaks of feeling a sense of freedom from any restrictions, "In that moment it was suddenly as if all fetters were cast off."[58] For at least a moment or two the toils of one's learning, the effort and stringency of one's practices, the endless stream of frustrations are left behind as understanding emerges. Kao momentarily at least transcends his limitations. Such an experience was, however, for Kao only a momentary insight. The actual goal of sagehood was yet distant.

In 1593 when Kao was banished to Chieh-yang[ar], he once again found himself ill at ease. He said that his mind had become agitated again. Thus the previous insight in which all bindings were said to have dropped off was an experience of the past. Kao commented in his autobiography, "Principle and desire waged battle upon battle without peaceful resolution within my mind."[59] The inner struggles that took place on this journey are apparent in both the K'un hsüeh chi and the travel journal San shih chi[as], "Recollections of the Three Seasons."[60] In his travel journal Kao singles out what he considers to be several crucial points of struggle. After arriving in Chieh-yang and taking up the responsibilities of his office he states, "Since I set out on this journey my outlook has already changed three times."[61] The word "outlook," shou shih[at], might also be translated as disposition or bearing though the sense of the word "outlook" conveys Kao's understanding and perspective of his own cultivation.

One of these turning points for Kao occurs in the setting of the Liu-ho Tower[au] in discussions with several acquaintances.[62] In this setting the night before he was to travel on Kao speaks of being unable to rest content or to share in the good times with his friends. He describes an awareness of an inner struggle in which the emergence of a "vague subtlety," yu yün[av] was being hindered,[63] and of his distinct feeling of disharmony with his natural surroundings.[64] He confessed that he had been depressed for successive days.[65] One of his acquaintances had asked him to describe the nature of the original substance, pen t'i and he had been unable to give an adequate response. The nadir was reached the night of parting at the Liu-ho Tower. A resolve was made to struggle again, to set up a schedule of rigid discipline, to break the binding force felt within. Continuing his journey on board a boat Kao stated, "I sat in silence deeply examining myself. I knew that the former effort had not been complete and [called for] a complete change of outlook."[66] This resolve by Kao changed a time of spiritual anguish into one of resolute struggle. The result of this struggle is a further example of the concept of transcendence in Kao's cultivation experiences.

The discipline that followed was rigorous according to the K'un hsüeh chi, morning and evening study interspersed with lengthy periods of quiet-sitting.[67] The result was a new breakthrough to understanding far more penetrating than Kao's previous experiences.

"I passed by T'ing-chou[aw] and traveled on by land until I reached an inn.[68] The inn had a small tower. To the front

were mountains, to the rear a nearby rushing stream.  I
climbed the tower and was very much at ease.  In my hand I
held a book of the two Ch'eng brothers.  Quite by chance I
saw a saying by Ming-tao[ax], 'In the midst of the ten-thousand
affairs and the hundred thousand weapons "joy still exists
though water is my drink and a bent arm [my pillow]."[69]
Changes all exist within man, while in reality there is not
a single affair (<u>ch'i shih wu i shih</u>)[ay].'[70]  I suddenly
realized this and said, 'It really is like this, in reality
there is not a single affair!'  There was singleness of
thought (<u>i nien</u>)[az] and all entanglements were broken off.
Suddenly it was as if a load of a hundred pounds had fallen
to the ground in an instant.  It was as if a flash of
lightning had penetrated the body and pierced the intell-
igence.  Subsequently I was merged with the Great Transformation[71] until there was no differentiation.  And yet even
further there was no partition between Heaven and man,
exterior and interior.  At this point I saw that the six
points[72] were all my mind, 'frame of the body' (<u>ch'iang tzu</u>)[ba]
was their field and 'square inch of space' (<u>i fang shou</u>)[bb]
was their original seat.[73]  But in terms of their spiritual
and luminous character, no location can actually be spoken
of."[74]

Kao thus experienced a sense of oneness with all things, a oneness
defined in terms of a common underlying principle within the nature
of all things.  He describes this awareness as seeing all things within himself and himself as the boundary of all things.  A new perspective was revealed to Kao for he had suddenly moved beyond the confine-
ment of his previous situation.  Such an experience might well be
spoken of as a transcendent perspective.  Kao himself refers to the
experience as his "enlightenment," <u>wu</u>[bc], a word and concept with which
Kao had felt quite uncomfortable prior to his own experience.  He
stated that he "ordinarily despised scholars who discussed enlightenment with grand display."[75]  Such scholars for Kao would be the
extreme left wing followers of Wang Yang-ming, the anathema of the
Tung-lin affiliates.  With his own "enlightenment," however, he came
to accept the possibility of such an experience within the process of
cultivation though the emphasis remains, however, on the disciplined
process of cultivation.  The "enlightenment" is not an end in itself
for Kao.  It is a very brief glimpse into the nature of things, a view
which for a few moments sees things in their unity and wholeness.

The examples I have chosen suggest an element of transcendence in
Kao's self-cultivation when transcendence is understood to be a breakthrough into a new perspective and an overcoming of certain previous
limitations.  Such a sense of transcendence seems particularly
suggestive of religious dimension within the context of self-
cultivation.  Transcendence is an important part of Kao's cultivation
experiences.  It offers for Kao an insight towards the goal to which
his efforts are directed, the nature of sagehood itself.

<u>An Element of Personal Faith</u>
        In addition to the experiences of transcendence Kao speaks
of what appears to be a new found relation for himself with certain
elements of his own Confucian tradition.  In speaking of this relation

in the K'un hsüeh chi Kao states that he has come to "truly believe"
particular aspects of his tradition.  The phrase "truly believe,"
shih hsin[bd] is suggestive of a type of relationship between participant
and tradition and as such warrants our careful consideration.

The references to shih hsin occur in the final sections of
the K'un hsüeh chi where Kao discusses principles central to his
tradition.

"In 1606 I came to truly believe in the principle of Mencius
that human nature is good.  This nature is not of the old or
of the new, **not** of the sagely or of the ordinary, for Heaven,
earth and man are one.  It is only on the highest grade that
[nature] is pure, clear and without shadows and that one is
a person of truth and integrity.  The next grade is entirely
dependent upon the effort of learning.[76]  If a single speck
of dust intervenes, it might as well be ten-thousand li[be].
This is the reason that Mencius spoke of the medicine that
causes a reaction."[77]

The belief in the goodness of the human nature would certainly seem to
be one of the most obvious beliefs that Kao could hold.  Perhaps more
is intended in the statement, however, than an acceptance of the belief
if by such an acceptance is meant only an intellectual recognition of
the validity of Mencius' principle.

"In 1607 I came to truly believe in [the principle of]
Master Ch'eng's, 'the hawk flies and fish swim,'[78] and also
[Mencius'], 'you must work at it.'[79]  What is called nature
is everything that is from the spontaneity of Heaven, not
from the effort of man.  'A hawk flies and fish swim,' who
caused this to be?  'Do not forget it, but also do not
assist it';[80] this is still the admonition to those who
study.  But in the case of the true primary substance (pen
t'i] that unceasingly flows and moves, overflows and dis-
perses, diffuses and spreads both in ancient times and the
present, where can it be forgotten or assisted?  Therefore
'one must work at it.'  Consider for example trees and
plants; their roots, sprouts, flowers and fruits change
and transform of their own, yet they are cared for, watered
and fostered.  If in the hard work of learning, one leaves
everything to spontaneity nothing will get done, no change
or transformation will be accomplished and there will not
even be any spontaneity."[81]

Kao relates his understanding in the year 1607 to two concepts, "the hawk flies and fish swim" from Master Ch'eng and "you must
work at it" from Mencius.  This understanding expressed as shih hsin
is of the utmost importance to his self-cultivation.  Kao's discussion
of quietude, ching[bf], and quiet sitting, ching tso, stresses both a
kind of spontaneity and yet also a need for strict discipline.  The
difference is expressed in these two short passages.  That "the hawk
flies and fish swim" is because of the spontaneity of Heaven, not
man's effort.  Trees and plants grow on their own and yet men need to
care for and cultivate them, i.e. work at them.  This act of assisting,
of helping along, is essential from Kao's point of view.  If only one

accepts the spontaneous nothing will come to fruition.  The nature
must be nurtured and developed.  The cultivation of sagehood for Kao
must be characterized by this same kind of balance between the careful
cultivation and the spontaneous emergence of the goodness of the
nature.  Much more could be said of Kao's understanding of the cultivation process but what is of interest here is the manner in which he
holds such understanding.  He continues to describe his relation as
one of true belief.

> "It was in 1611 I came to truly believe in the Ta hsüeh[bg] and
> its principle of 'knowing the root.'  This is fully recorded
> in another work."[82]

The principle of "knowing the root," chih pen[bh], became a
part of Kao's belief.  This was the culmination of a long struggle
with the Ta hsüeh.  Kao records earlier in the K'un hsüeh chi that
when he was younger he had worked on "knowing the root."[83]  In
addition Kao dealt with the Ta hsüeh in some detail in several essays.[84]
In the Ku pen Ta hsüeh t'i tz'u[bi] Kao summarized some of the contro-
versy over the interpretation of the Ta hsüeh.  He suggested that
various rearrangements of the text by Ch'eng I, Ch'eng Hao and Chu
Hsi had not settled the debate over the text nor had they settled his
own doubts.[85]  He confessed that the problems of the Ta hsüeh had
pressed upon him for many years.[86]  Through his own rearrangement of
the text,[87] however, he was able to resolve his doubts.  This resolution leads to the possibility that in 1611 he can state his shih hsin
or true belief.

The final entry in the K'un hsüeh chi concerns Kao's belief
in the Chung yung[bj], the Mean.

> "In 1612 I came to truly believe the principle of the Chung
> yung.  Most surely words cannot describe this way.  Master
> Ch'eng called it the principle of Heaven, [Wang] Yang-ming
> called it innate knowing.  Neither, however, equals the two
> words 'centrality' and 'normality.'  'Centrality' is what is
> suitable and fitting, 'normality' is what is ordinary and
> dependable.  If even a slight transgression takes place,
> nothing will be suitable and fitting.  If there is only a
> slight bit of artiface or contrivance, it will not be
> ordinary and dependable.  It is this way with the substance
> and it is this way with moral effort."[88]

What he had come to see, he said words could not describe.  Kao
reiterates what others had called this state, but found the Mean to be
for himself the most adequate description.  The Mean resembles a
delicate balance which when achieved emerges as the core of all things.
Either through shortcomings or through artificiality the Mean may be
missed and the awareness of a fundamental unity cast aside.  The autobiography draws towards its conclusion with Kao's statement of belief
in the Mean.  Kao had come to believe in what he said was inexpress-
able though he chose to call it by the name Chung yung, the Mean.

It does not seem adequate in the context of these passages
to define Kao's belief as either an intellectual or emotional acceptance.  The inadequacy of such a definition becomes clearer in under-

standing the depth of Kao's commitment and the object of his belief.
To represent the type of commitment involved in the phrase <u>shih hsin</u>,
the word "faith" might be suggested in place of "true belief."  In
substituting the word "faith" for "true belief" there is no intention
of emphasizing a relation based upon a blind acceptance of something
that is not known with accuracy.  Such an understanding of faith would
emphasize no more than the acceptance or unacceptance of a given
premise and methods of proof.  These may well be quite secondary concerns to the dimensions of faith.  Frederick Streng's treatment of
faith is provocative for he sees the limitations that have been placed
upon the use of faith and yet he is aware of its potentiality as a
meaningful category descriptive of the religious dimension of human
life.[89]  Faith is spoken of as "a way of living, not merely a way of
thinking, that places man's everyday existence in the context of an
eternal reality."[90]  It can be described as a kind of relationship
established between an individual and what he regards as true.  The
individual who is able to "live in" or maintain such a relation is he
who has faith.  Such an individual may be described as living
authentically.

The object of Kao's faith is what is considered to be true
or authentic, man's true nature or <u>hsing</u> sought through the efforts of
self-cultivation.  It is not a faith in the "ideas" of Mencius, nor is
it a faith in the "principles" of the <u>Ta hsüeh</u> or the <u>Chung yung</u>.  It
is a faith in these works only so far as they relate to the emergence
of the true nature itself.  The activity described is not propositional
in structure; it is not a belief in "ideas" to be accepted for
intellectual, emotional or moral value.  Rather faith is directed
towards precisely that which is considered true, man's nature itself
which emerges in the state of sagehood.  Through such an expression of
faith Kao partakes of an authentic life.  The act of declaring such
faith reaffirms Kao's relation to the goal towards which he is directed.
He moves back into relation with the goal.

Kao's use of the phrase <u>shih hsin</u>, true belief or faith, is
suggestive of a broad range of religious dimension.  It raises the
question as to what degree the Confucian tradition, whether expressed
in intellectual activity or moral concern, was an intensely personal
religious faith for individual participants of the tradition.

<u>The Religious Dimension, Its Application and Breadth</u>
Kao's quest for sagehood is characterized by resolute effort
and determination within a broad range of activity and thought.  We
have for the purposes of space limited ourselves in this paper to a
presentation of several of many possible elements that might make up
the religious dimension of Neo-Confucianism.  The elements we have
discussed, however, should be sufficient to indicate the import of
Neo-Confucianism for any attempt to deal in a broad way with the
nature and definition of religious phenomena in the Chinese tradition.

The types of activity and thought engaged in by Kao in his
attempt to fulfill the goal of sagehood may well indicate the possible
range of religious activity and thought.  As a working methodology for
the study of the Confucian tradition no activity ought to be excluded
a priori from the question of the religious dimension regardless of
what degree such activity or thought may at first appear to be

-22-

exclusive of religious structure.  A particular type of activity or
thought cannot be considered non-religious as such until the structure
within which this activity or thought occurs has been investigated and
understood.  Thus concerns quite often spoken of as humanistic in fact
possess a religious dimension if such concerns exist within a larger
context identified as religious.  If we identify the goal of sagehood
as possessing religious structure because of a soteriological presupposition or expressions of transcendence and faith, than the
activity and thought that make up the cultivation process take on a
new dimension.  Activity and thought in the path towards sagehood may
then quite correctly be spoken of as religious activity and thought.

        The study and understanding of Confucianism, both Classical
Confucianism and Neo-Confucianism, is still a challenge for the
Historian of Religion for the tradition as a whole is only with some
difficulty placed among the religious traditions of the world.  Not so
distant echoes can still be heard of the charge that Confucianism more
properly belongs to a category of humanism devoid of religious structure.[91]  C. K. Yang, for example, raises this problem as a continuing
issue in the study of Confucianism.  It is certainly noteworthy that
he sees the nature of the problem, however, he concludes by merely
pointing to what he calls "religious elements" of the tradition,
elements which most significantly appear tangential to the body of
Confucian teachings.  This is the case, for example, in Yang's discussion of supernatural factors involved in the examination system.[92]
Though no definitive answer can be given, the question might at least
be raised as to why the "religious elements" must be confined to the
sacrifice to the God of Literature?  Though this question hinges on a
proper understanding of the dimensions of state orthodoxy and the in-
terplay between the state orthodoxy and the voluntary orthodoxy of
individual thinkers, the possibility can at least be suggested that
the content of the examination may possess particular religious concerns.  To what degree is the ideal of sagehood implicit within the
content of the examinations?  This is something that might well be
investigated further.  I have no intention of idealizing the examination system by suggesting that all those who were involved in the
system had as their purpose the attainment of sagehood.  And yet the
sage is one who expresses himself through human relations, who affirms
the life process.  The most ordinary of activities expressive of human
and societal relations and bonds are not to be easily divorced from
the Confucian religious dimension.

        Based upon the present evidence it is not possible to specu-
late on the nature of the entire Confucian tradition, nor the range of
Neo-Confucianism for that matter.  In the case of Kao P'an-lung, however, we do have an example of the role of religious dimension in his
thought and practice.  He consciously centers his own focus on the
quest for sagehood, a process to be characterized as a self-
transformation into what is considered authentic existence.  Such
authentic existence is the realization of one's true nature and thus a
sense of unity with the Principle, li, within all things.  The quest
is considered soteriological.  This does not deny the role of humanistic concerns, but simply places them in their proper perspective.
First and foremost is a religious concern.  The degree to which
thoughts and activities center around and upon the understanding of
one's true nature is the degree to which Kao's life can be charac-

terized and spoken of as religious.

     The manner in which activities relate to the goal of sage-
hood indicates not only the primacy of a soteriological concern, but
also a comprehensiveness in the religious dimension.  For Kao the
religious dimension is not only the goal of sagehood, but also the
vast range of activities and thought that become a part of the orientation towards sagehood.  The religious dimension thus has a sense of
thoroughness as it manifests itself in various modes of Kao's thought
and action.  We have seen that the element of transcendence is an
important part of Kao's cultivation experience.  He also expresses
"true belief" or what might best be called "faith" in the authenticity
of his own tradition.  Each and every encounter and activity can serve
as a way of approaching the understanding of the true nature.  In the
seriousness of the question before him, Kao displays a life marked by
a thorough-going sense of the religious.

Footnotes

$^{1}$*Mencius* 6B/2.

$^{2}$W. T. deBary, "Neo-Confucian Cultivation and the 17th Century 'Enlightenment,'" Draft Manuscript, Conference on 17th Century Chinese Thought, September 1970.

$^{3}$Chu Hsi and Lü Tsu-ch'ien, *Reflections on Things at Hand*, trans. W. T. Chan (New York: Columbia University Press, 1967); see also Chu Hsi *Chin ssu lu chi chieh*$^{bk}$, commentary by Chang Pai-hsing (Taipei: Shih chieh shu chü, 1967).

$^{4}$Chan, p. 35; *Chin ssu lu*, p. 29.

$^{5}$Chan, p. 307; *Chin ssu lu*, p. 345.

$^{6}$Chan, p. 308; *Chin ssu lu*, p. 346.

$^{7}$Rodney L. Taylor, "The Cultivation of Sagehood as a Religious Goal in Neo-Confucianism: A Study of Selected Writings of Kao P'an-lung (1562-1626)" (Ph.D. dissertation, Columbia University, 1974).

$^{8}$W. T. deBary has provided much of the foundation for the understanding of the ideal of sagehood as it emerges in the Sung and flowers in the Ming. See in particular W. T. deBary, ed., *Self and Society in Ming Thought* (New York: Columbia University Press, 1970); W. T. deBary, "Introduction," *Self and Society in Ming Thought*, ed. W. T. deBary (New York: Columbia University Press, 1970), pp. 1-28; W. T. deBary, "Neo-Confucian Cultivation."

$^{9}$Chan, pp. 74-75; *Chin ssu lu*, p. 71.

$^{10}$W. T. Chan, *A Source Book in Chinese Philosophy* (Princeton: Princeton University Press, 1963, pb. 1969), p. 523.

$^{11}$Chan, *Reflections*, p. 85; *Chin ssu lu*, p. 85.

$^{12}$Chan, *Reflections*, pp. 76-77; *Chin ssu lu*, pp. 73-75.

$^{13}$Chan, *Source Book*, pp. 523-24.

$^{14}$deBary, "Introduction," pp. 8-12.

$^{15}$For a discussion of the Ch'eng-Chu position in the early Ming see W. T. Chan, "The Ch'eng-Chu School of the Early Ming," in *Self and Society in Ming Thought*, ed. W. T. deBary (New York: Columbia University Press, 1970), pp. 29-52.

$^{16}$See Heinrich Busch, "The Tung-lin Academy and Its Political and Philosophical Significance," (Ph.D. dissertation, Columbia University, 1954), pp. 166-171, 177-182 *et passim*. Also published in *Monumenta Serica* XIV (1949-1955), pp. 1-163. See also Taylor, pp. 26-40, 75-83.

$^{17}$W. T. deBary, "Individualism and Humanitarianism in Late Ming

Thought," in <u>Self and Society in Ming Thought</u>, ed. W. T. deBary (New York: Columbia University Press, 1970), p. 171.

[18]See Hucker's article for a discussion of the Tung-lin Party. Charles Hucker, "The Tung-lin Movement of the Late Ming Period," in <u>Chinese Thought and Institutions</u>, ed. John Fairbank (Chicago: University of Chicago Press, 1964), pp. 151-62.

[19]For a general review of the role and type of academies existent during the Ming, see John Meskill, "Academies and Politics in the Ming Dynasty," in <u>Chinese Government in Ming Times: Seven Studies</u>, ed. Charles Hucker (New York: Columbia University Press, 1969), pp. 149-174.

[20]Busch, p. 115.

[21]Taylor, pp. 26-40.

[22]Huang Tsung-hsi, <u>Ming ju hsüeh an</u>[bl] (Taipei: Shih chieh shu chü, 1965), p. 613.

[23]See <u>ibid</u>. p. 627 and Jung Chao-Tsu[bm] <u>Ming tai ssu hsiang shih</u>[bn] (Taipei: K'ai shen shu tien, 1969), pp. 309-310.

[24]Kao P'an-lung, <u>K'un hsüeh chi</u> (Recollections of the Toils of Learning), hereafter referred to as <u>KHC</u>, found in <u>Kao tzu i shu</u>[bo] (Literary Remains of Kao P'an-lung), Ch'en Lung-cheng[bp] ed., 1876 ed., 3/13b. See Busch, p. x for a brief discussion of the <u>Kao tzu i shu</u> hereafter referred to as <u>KTIS</u>. <u>KHC</u> was written in 1614 according to the chronological biography. See <u>Kao Chung-hsien kung nien p'u</u>[bq] (Chronological Biography of Kao P'an-lung), Hua Yun-ch'eng[br] ed., appendix to <u>KTIS</u>, 15b. Hereafter referred to as <u>nien p'u</u>. The title of <u>KHC</u> is an allusion to <u>Analects</u>, 16/9.

[25]The provincial examination was passed in 1582, <u>nien p'u</u>, 3b.

[26]<u>KHC</u>, 13b.

[27]Ibid.

[28]<u>nien p'u</u>, 3b-4a.

[29]The diary was to serve as a record for proper and improper actions and attitudes experienced throughout the course of each day. Ibid.

[30]<u>KHC</u>, 13b.

[31]Frederick J. Streng, <u>Understanding Religious Man</u> (Belmont, California: Dickenson Publishing Company, Inc., 1969), pp. 4-5.

[32]These criteria of religious experience are first, a response to what is experienced as Ultimate Reality, second, a total response of the total being, third, intensity, and fourth, the imperative to issue in action. Joachim Wach, <u>The Comparative Study of Religion</u> (New York: Columbia University Press, 1958, pb. ed. 1966), Chapter II, "The Nature of Religious Experience," pp. 27-58. Wach has also discussed

this issue in a chapter entitled, "Universals in Religion."  Joachim
Wach, _Types of Religious Experience Christian and Non-Christian_
(Chicago: University of Chicago Press, 1970), pp. 30-47.

[33]Ninian Smart has commented at some length on the approach finding
what he feels to be certain weaknesses in Wach's emphasis upon religious
experience as the salient characteristic of religion.  See in particular Ninian Smart, _The Philosophy of Religion_ (New York: Random House,
1970), pp. 4-5, 7.

[34]Streng, pp. 4-5.

[35]Ibid., p. 4.

[36]Wach, _Comparative Study_, pp. 30-32.

[37]I will confine my remarks here to the Ch'eng-Chu understanding of
man's nature rather than introduce the role of _hsin_[bs], mind.  Essential,
however, to both the _hsing_ and _hsin_ for the Ch'eng-chu and Wang Yang-
ming traditions respectively is the underlying Principle, _li_.

[38]As a second characteristic of his definition of religion, Streng
discusses what he calls "effective power."  According to this position
a religious tradition contains its own effective power to realize its
highest goals.  It is in a sense "practical," for it possesses the
potentiality for transformation.  Streng, p. 5.

[39]Wach, _Comparative Study_, p. 36.

[40]_KHC_, 17b.

[41]Wach, _Comparative Study_, p. 32.

[42]Ibid., p. 35.

[43]Ninian Smart discusses the term "transcendent" as a possible
approach towards the characterization of religious phenomena only to
reject its use on the grounds that it involves theological presuppositions and value judgments.  Smart, pp. 30-31.

[44]Kao P'an-lung, _Shui chü chi_ (Recollections of the Water Dwelling),
_KTIS_, 10/48b-49a.  There is no information on the date of the text.
The chronological biography states only that the Water Dwelling was
built in the year 1598 (_nien p'u_, p. 12a.).

[45]_Shui chü chi_, KTIS 10/48b.

[46]The Primal Harmony, _t'ai ho_[bt], is similar to what Wilhelm trans-
lates as the Great Harmony, _ta ho_[bu], in the T'uan Chuan[bv], Commentary
of the Decision, to the Ch'ien[bw] hexagram.  See Richard Wilhelm, trans.,
_The I Ching or Book of Changes_, Vol. II, Bollingen Series XIX, 2nd. ed.
(New York: Pantheon Books, 1964), p. 4.

[47]Flowing Forces, _hao ch'i_[bx], is a reference to _hao jan chih ch'i_[by],
_Mencius_, 2A/2 understood as the flowing and activating force of the
universe.

[48] Gate of the Inexhaustible, _wu ch'iung chih men_[bz] occurs in
Chuang Tzu. Chuang Tzu[ca], _Chuang tzu chi shih_[cb] (Taipei: Shih chieh
shu chü, 1967), p. 174. See also Chuang Tzu, _The Complete Works of
Chuang Tzu_, trans., Burton Watson (New York: Columbia University Press,
1968), p. 120.

[49] _Shui chü chi_, _KTIS_ 10/49a.

[50] Kao P'an-lung, _K'o lou chi_ (Recollections of the Suitable Loft),
_KTIS_, 10/49a-50a. As with the _Shui chü chi_ there is no information on
the date of this text. According to the chronological biography, there
is no great separation in time between the building of the Water Dwelling and the addition of a loft to the structure. They are both recorded under the entry for 1598 (_nien p'u_, 12a).

[51] _K'o lou chi_, _KTIS_ 10/49b.

[52] _K'o lou chi_, _KTIS_ 10/50a.

[53] Quiet-sitting is a form of meditation practiced by Kao and other
Neo-Confucians. For Kao the purpose of quiet-sitting was to see into
his true nature or the ground of his nature which he describes as _pen
t'i_, the original substance. _KHC_, 14a. Kao has several writings
dealing specifically with the practice of quiet-sitting. _Ching tso
shuo_[cc] (A Discussion of Quiet-Sitting), _KTIS_, 3/19b-20b; _Ching tso
shuo huo_[cd] (A Later Discussion of Quiet-Sitting), _KTIS_, 3/20b-21a;
_Fu ch'i kuei_[ce] (Rules for 'Returning in Seven'), _KTIS_, 3/18b-19a.
See Taylor, pp. 112-129, 275-280 for study and translation of these
texts.

[54] A paraphrase of a line from the Ch'ien Hexagram, Wen-yen
commentary to nine-for-the-second-place. See _Chou I_[cf], _Ssu pu pei yao_
ed.[cg] (Shanghai: Chung hua shu chü, n.d.), Vol. I, 2b; Wilhelm, Vol.
II, p. 12.

[55] See Busch, pp. 115, 128-129, 165-166 for a discusion of the term
_tang hsia_.

[56] _KHC_, 14a.

[57] It is obvious in the context that this relation between _ch'eng_
and _hsing_ in the response of the nature is of great importance to Kao
for it illustrates the immediacy of the true nature and the ability to
respond with the true nature.

[58] _KHC_, 14a.

[59] _KHC_, 14b.

[60] Kao P'an-lung, _San shih chi_ (Recollections of Three Seasons),
_KTIS_, 10/25b-48a.

[61] _San shih chi_, _KTIS_, 10/37a.

[62] _San shih chi_, _KTIS_, 10/27b-28b; _KHC_, 14b-15a.

[63]San shih chi, KTIS, 10/30a.

[64]KHC, 14b. The natural surroundings play an unusually important role in Kao's life of cultivation. There is a sense in which they are a measure of his cultivation for if he can feel a rapport with the surrounding then the cultivation appears to be acceptable. The role of aesthetic sensitivity and its relation to the cultivation process is discussed in Taylor, pp. 75-102, 159-164, et passim.

[65]San shih chi, KTIS, 10/30a.

[66]Ibid.

[67]KHC, 15a.

[68]T'ing-chou is located in the western corner of Fukien near its border with Kiangsi. A detailed account is given in San shih chi, KTIS, 10/34a; nien p'u 8a.

[69]Analects, 7/15.

[70]This saying is found in Ch'eng Hao and Ch'eng I, Erh Ch'eng ch'üan shu[ch], Ssu pu pei yao ed. (Shanghai: Chung hua shu chü, n.d.), Vol. I, 6/3a. The phrase wu i shih, "without a single affair," is significant for the emphasis placed upon an openness or emptiness as a description of the nature of the mind.

[71]Increase and decrease of yin[ci] and yang[cj].

[72]Six points are north, south, east, west, zenith and nadir.

[73]The discussion of the "frame of the body" and the "square inch of space" refers back to Kao's struggles with self-cultivation early after setting his aspirations upon the goal of sagehood. He tries first to cultivate the state of ching[ck], reverence or seriousness, but is unsuccessful because he limits his understanding of mind to a "square inch of space," i.e. the heart as an organ. Only after finding mind explained as filling the "frame of the body" does he reach a measure of contentment. KHC, 13b.

[74]KHC, 15b-16a.

[75]KHC, 16a.

[76]There is an allusion here to Analects, 16/9 already alluded to in the title K'un hsüeh chi. The passage refers to the differing capabilities of various persons in the learning process. Kao is distinguishing between the highest level who are born wise and those who have to realize their natures through learning.

[77]KHC, 17a.

[78]Locus classicus, Shih Ching[cl], III/1/5 (Mao number 239).

[79]Mencius, 2A/2. I have followed the rendering of D.C. Lau.

Mencius, trans., D.C. Lau (Baltimore, Maryland: Penguin Books, 1970),
p. 78.

[80]Mencius, 2A/2.

[81]KHC, 17a-b.

[82]KHC, 17b.

[83]KHC, 14a.

[84]Kao's work on the Ta hsüeh is recorded in three separate writings: Ku pen ta hsüeh t'i tz'u, KTIS 3/1a-2b, a discussion of the
problems of the text; Ta hsüeh shou chang yüeh i[cm], KTIS 3/2b-4a, Kao's
rearrangement of the text; and Ta hsüeh shou chang kuang i[cn], KTIS,
3/4a-12b, a compilation of what others have said about the text.

[85]KTIS, 3/1a-b. Kao's greatest doubts focused upon problems in
Chu Hsi's rearrangement of the text to permit ko wu[co], investigation
of things, and chih chih[cp], extension of knowledge, to retain primacy
in the steps of cultivation.

[86]KTIS, 3/1a.

[87]Ta hsüeh shou chang yüeh i, KTIS, 3/2b-4a.

[88]KHC, 17b.

[89]Streng, pp. 53-55.

[90]Streng, p. 54.

[91]C. K. Yang, Religion in Chinese Society (Berkeley: University of
California Press, 1961), pp. 3-6.

[92]Ibid., pp. 265-272.

a 聖　聖人
b 堯
c 舜　宋
d 宋
e 近　思　錄
f 朱　熹
g 呂　祖　謙
h 張　載
i 程　頤
j 程　顥
k 明
l 高　攀　龍
m 仁
n 性
o 理
p 天　理
q 王　陽　明
r 程　朱
s 良　知
t 東　林
u 王　艮
v 泰　州
w 顏　鈞
x 羅　汝　芳
y 東　林　書　院
z 東　林　黨

aa 顧　憲　成
ab 李　贄
ac 黃　宗　羲
ad 困　學　記
ae 志　於　學　以　為　聖　人
af 志
ag 李　元　沖
ah 無　錫
ai 日　金　監　篇
aj 水　居　記
ak 可　樓　記
al 可
am 靜　坐
an 本　體
ao 易　經
ap 誠
aq 當　下　陽
ar 揭　陽　時　記
as 三　時　勢　記　塔
at 手　和
au 六　幽　蘊　州
av 汀　州　道
aw 汀
ax 明　道
ay 其　實　無　一　事
az 一　念

|  | |  | |
|------|------|------|------|
| ba | 腔子 | ca | 莊子 |
| bb | 方寸 | cb | 莊子集釋 |
| bc | 悟 | cc | 靜坐說 |
| bd | 實信 | cd | 靜坐說後 |
| be | 里 | ce | 復七規 |
| bf | 靜 | cf | 周易 |
| bg | 大學 | cg | 四部備要 |
| bh | 知本 | ch | 二程全書 |
| bi | 古本大學題詞 | ci | 陰 |
| bj | 中庸 | cj | 陽 |
| bk | 近思錄集解 | ck | 敬 |
| bl | 明儒學案 | cl | 詩經 |
| bm | 容肇祖 | cm | 大學絢義 |
| bn | 明代思想史 | cn | 大學首章 |
| bo | 高子遺書 | co | 格物 |
| bp | 陳龍正 | cp | 致知 |
| bq | 高忠憲公年譜 | | |
| br | 華允誠 | | |
| bs | 心和 | | |
| bt | 太和 | | |
| bu | 大和 | | |
| bv | 象傳 | | |
| bw | 乾 | | |
| bx | 浩氣 | | |
| by | 浩然之氣 | | |
| bz | 無窮之門 | | |

THE GENESIS OF GODS IN TAIWANESE FOLK RELIGION:
A PRELIMINARY ANALYSIS

Philip C. Baity

University of California, Berkeley

The origins of Chinese gods have long been of interest to
the Chinese; there exist countless legends detailing their exploits.
Some of these legends have been integrated into works such as the
Feng-shen Yen-i or "Metamorphosis of the gods," a famous work of the
17th century.  Others may be found in the form of temple pamphlets
which even today in Taiwan are published by local temples and distribu-
ted to the public; still others are recorded in the form of local legends.

What many of these legends share in common is their insist-
ence that in their origins the gods were, with few exceptions, the
canonized spirits of eminent men, officials, local heros, and immortals
who were worshipped, and in some cases officially canonized by the
Imperial Board of Rites to thank and reward them for their loyal and
virtuous deeds in the service of the nation and its people. [1]  Together these gods formed a spiritual bureaucracy, mirroring that of
the Imperial government, which was relatively uniform and enduring
across the Empire.

In contrast to the official pantheon of which very few informants have any precise notion at all, there exists another, still
extant today, composed of gods who are worshipped in ordinary temples,
and shrines scattered throughout the countryside.  Many of these gods
are of merely local significance, and are not found at all in the
official pantheon.

The main difference between the two systems lies in the fact
that, unlike many of the official gods or ancestors, the popular gods
were always worshipped in expectation of some immediate material bene-
fit in return.

To understand the difference in character of the community
god as opposed to the gods in the official bureaucracy, it is necessary
to understand the reason for reciprocal and non-reciprocal worship and
the impact that this has on the promotion of the gods in the two systems.  The notion of reciprocity also makes clear the difference that
exists between the god and the ghost, the ancestor and the immortal.
However, few attempts have been made to define with greater clarity or
precision the native concepts such as god (shen), immortal (hsien),
Buddha (fo), or ancestor.  In fact, the analysis of these terms has
been fettered by a popular assumption that these different classes of
beings were quite similar to one another.

Some researchers have affirmed that in fact it is impossible
to draw a clear line between gods and ancestors (Shryock; 1931:57).  In
part this confusion is shared by the Taiwanese, who are prone to endow
both gods and ghosts with human characteristics.  In the legendary
accounts we find not only that gods are attributed the same desires and
cravings as men, but that their life style is similar in all respects,
even to the point of their having wives and children (Lin; 1962:101).

In the popular stories about ghosts they too are found to have children
(Eberhard: 1970:70).

Yet not enough attention has been directed on the fact that
there are also profound differences in the folk conception of these
different classes of spiritual beings.  Ghosts are visualized as being
the opposite from gods.  There are important differences in the manner
in which the different spirits are treated in ritual, and a quite different rationale for worship in the different cases.

The Imperial government expressed its approbation of eminent
citizens, by granding them posthumous titles thanking them for a virtuous administration, or for deeds of valor and loyalty; this process
is called kan en hsieh tê (feeling thanks for favors and virtue).  The
feeling which the government tried to instill in the people is much
closer to the feeling of children towards their parents as espoused by
orthodox Confucianism.  Their debt could never be paid in full, nor
was it performed in expectation of any return, rather it was almost
always the expression of gratitude for favors already rendered. [2]
The government disapproved of worship of spirits for material return.

Unlike his counterpart in legend, the "community god" always
exists in relationship to a group of worshippers.  He has a well defined personality, even with respect to other gods of the same name or
type.  Each god is an individual, having a status in the local hierarchy of gods which is his by virtue of his own achievements, his popularity with the people in a given community, and not dependent upon
the whim or fancy of the Imperial Board of Rites.  The popularity of
a deity was the result of his efficacy in answering the prayers of the
worshipper, and the prayers themselves were often attempts to cajole,
persuade, or force the deity to perform some act or favor.  The deity
has a good reason to respond, because his position in the hierarchy is
determined by his efficacy alone.

For a deity to become sufficiently popular to have a temple
erected in his honor (and to become and remain a symbol of a community)
he must be "public" and "efficacious."

He must be able to produce efficacious miracles in response
to the worshipper's prayers.  He may cure diseases, bring wealth, luck
or children to his believers, or bring disaster to an enemy.  In addition, the deity must be able to demonstrate this efficacy in the public sphere.  His efficacy, however well established, will not lead to
popularity unless he is able and willing to make it available to the
community as a whole.  Many efficacious spirits are either unwilling
or unable to become public spirits.

There are many reasons why a particular spirit may not qualify for the role of a public efficacious spirit.  Foremost of these is
that he may be an ancestor, that is, a spirit who is unwilling to respond efficaciously to the demands of any but his own descendants.

The patterns of reciprocity which obtain between an ancestor
and his descendants differ in three respects from those between a man
and a community god.  A man's ties to his descendants are private, and
exclusive; these ties are not strictly reciprocal, and they are long

term. [3]  A man's ties to his ancestors derives from the fact of his birth, and unless he is adopted into another lineage, this tie remains in effect all his life, and even beyond.  Because of this exclusive tie, worship directed to the ancestor, as well as benefits which might be expected to derive from him, are in normal circumstances restricted to direct descendants.

To worship another's ancestors is not only condemned as un-confucian, but it is futile as well, for the "ancestor" will not respond to the demands of a non-descendant so long as his own descendants honor their filial obligations to worship him and to continue the family line by having children, who will carry on the ancestral worship in their turn.

Community gods cannot in fact have been men with children as this would make them into ancestors, and would make them unable to provide efficacious benefits for non-descendants.

In this sense then, regardless of what the official legends state, a public community god must always be conceived of by worshippers as a spiritual being who has no direct ties with living descendants, i.e., a childless spirit or a "lonely ghost," or at least a person who has broken off the ties with his family.  This supposition will be borne out by examining the actual processes by which childless spirits come to be worshipped by the public, and how they came to be transformed into gods.

The absence of familial ties, as important as it is in understanding the public nature of the god and his willingness to reciprocate the worship that he receives, is itself not sufficient to explain the process of reciprocity which leads to the formation of deities. Gods are not the only beings, in fact, to suffer from an absence of familial ties.  They share this quality with hsien (immortals) and Buddhas.  The immortal frequently deserts the company of family and men, and having retreated to the wilderness, there produces the immortal foetus by the methods of nei tan, the "inner elixir."  But while men may respect immortals, they do not worship them, and immortals are rarely the objects of temple cults.

In his analysis of folktale themes, Eberhard (1970:69) rightfully pointed out that there was little reciprocity between men and immortals:  "Immortals are similar to deified persons but cannot be asked to do something mainly because they do not have temples where they can be reached.  Their use to mankind is limited to their own fancy and cannot be directed."  The reason that they do not have temples is, of course, explained by the fact that the immortals, having already compounded the immortal elixir by themselves, have nothing to gain from a relationship with men.  Moreover, because immortals are believed to remain alive in the world, they do not need descendants to carry on their ancestral worship.

Buddhas, too, are self-achieved (tzu tsai) beings whose position is not due to human assistance.  Although Buddhas are frequently enshrined in Buddhist temples, they and their temples are rarely the centers of community cults. [4]  Many townsmen do not believe that Buddhas are able or willing to help ordinary people, but the stated reasons for this vary.

Buddhas are believed by many informants to be too remote from worldly affairs and the interests of men to be able or willing to grant their prayers, and many people stated that they did not believe that Buddhas would accede to human demands because many humans were immoral in their eyes. One informant confessed that even if Buddhas did respond to human prayers, that they would be slower in doing so than would a god (shen).

Even Buddhist monks have told me that the Buddhas differed from the gods because they were not efficacious. "How could they be, they are mere statues of clay," said one monk, confirming the notion shared by many townsmen. [5]

Whatever the reason given by the folk, there is a distinct difference felt in the willingness or ability of the Buddha, god and immortal to reciprocate worship.

In essence the difference between them can be reduced to the fact that the god relies on human worship for his advancement in the spiritual bureaucracy, while the hsien (and the Buddhas) rely instead upon their own efforts and spiritual practices. Since neither the immortal or the Buddha depend upon the worship of men for their spiritual advancement, their willingness to reciprocate is also cast into doubt. For all practical purposes, the only other beings that can be shown to have a need for human worship and a willingness to reciprocate, are the lonely ghosts.

Not all ghosts have the potential to become objects of public worship because many of them are also ancestors. But it is recognized that there is one kind of ghost, the "lonely ghost," who is different from the rest, because he does not have descendants to worship him. They are often called "hungry ghosts," since they are lacking in food offerings.

Hungry ghosts present both a threat and an opportunity to the living community. They, like ancestors, are believed to be dangerous unless worshipped, and if ignored they too may wreak their vengeance upon the living, causing illness and death. Because they present a danger to men, it is incumbent upon the living to supply them with their needs, or to expel them from the confines of the community so that they will not create trouble. There is thus at the outset, a need to worship hungry ghosts which is independent, initially at least, from any considerations of reciprocity.

In addition, like god worship, ghost worship, whether undertaken individually or by large groups, is different in one respect at least, from ancestral worship, in that the links which are forged between the worshippers are not the natural private links of agnation which bind a worshipper to his ancestors. Instead they too are "public," because they bind unrelated people. [6] Having no descendants of their own, ghosts are also believed capable of granting the wishes of the worshipper.

Ghosts also have low moral standards (perhaps because they are accused of unfilial conduct), and are willing to accede to the most

immoral demands.  Because they are willing to grant any wish, from
luck in gambling to raining disease and disaster upon one's enemies,
ghost worship has remained popular in urban areas of Taiwan up to the
present day.

Thus it may be understood that gods, ghosts, and ancestors
live in the supernatural world, the ties of reciprocity between them
are different because in the one case they have broken the home ties
and are thus available to the public, in the other case they are not.

These relationships may be demonstrated in the following
diagram:

|  | still living<br>in this world | not living<br>in this world |
|---|---|---|
| fixed<br>home ties<br>'private' | men ⟵——— *Private* ———⟶ ancestors<br>reciprocity | |
| left home or<br>broke ties<br>'public' | Hsien<br>immortals | gods and<br>hungry ghosts |
| | Buddhas<br>neither 'in'<br>nor 'not in'<br>the world | |

*Public reciprocity* (diagonal arrow from ancestors/men toward gods and hungry ghosts)

Although community gods and ghosts share the need for human
worship in their spiritual ascent and both are willing to reciprocate
favors, there are fundamental differences between them.  Gods represent all that is good from the human point of view; they are attributed
long life, if not immortality, large families, wealth, food, power.
Ghosts, on the other hand, are believed to be deficient in all of these
qualities.

This separation, which is equivalent to the separation between
the yin and yang worlds, is symbolized through many differences in ritual.  One of these differences is the fact that gods are worshipped on
their birthday, while ancestors and ghosts are worshipped on their death
day.

If gods begin as hungry ghosts and are gradually transformed
into deities, the human agency is indispensible to this transformation.
The transformation is also necessary in order to remove the pollution,
and bad luck associated with death and childlessness. [7]

Since gods are attributed with the good things of life, and
ghosts with a lack of these things, the transmorgification of ghosts
into gods would require that at some point of the process, the ghost-
god  be endowed with those characteristics which would, so to speak,
mark the transition point of his career, from yin to yang being.  When
a ghost becomes a god a change is made on the date on which he is worshipped.  Gods and ghosts may also be provided with wives and children

by their worshippers at some point in their spiritual career. [8]

Although euhemeristic accounts of these ghosts and gods detail family life, these accounts may often be demonstrated to be late versions.

The case of the Taipei City God is an example of how a god may obtain a wife long after he has been installed as a god. In 1893, after this deity, called Pearly Ocean City God, had been in Taiwan for over a century, and some thirty years after he had been enshrined in a temple, the temple keeper, a certain Mr. Ao living in the area, thought that although the god had a great deal of spiritual efficacy, he did not have a wife; thinking that if he recommended a wife to the god, it would be pleased, he carried in a statue of a female spirit, and set it beside the god, and this was the origin of the City God's wife (Sokeirai: 316-317).

But this procedure for providing a spouse for the deity should not obscure the mechanisms by which community gods arise. To claim that a "hungry ghost" has children is a contradiction in terms and a violation of the logic of the cognitive system. In the case of a ghost which becomes a god, on the other hand, the attempt to attribute a family to the god is an attempt to maintain the coherence of the structure.

There is yet another reason why the gods might be attributed with families in the legendary accounts. The reason for this may have been an effort on the part of the government and the people alike to conceal the real nature and purpose of spirit worship. An attempt by assigning a pedigree to obscure the fact that it was the dead ghosts who were being worshipped, and that this was being done in expectation of material returns.

Stories stressing the heroic and virtuous nature of those spirits who do become gods serve to mask the true origins of the gods, who emerged from very different sources, indeed from the very antithesis of the canons of virtue and filial piety which they seemingly extol. They represent a strain of religious belief that is unorthodox and is condemned and persecuted by the authorities.

In most stories about the origins of the deities there are mixed elements stressing both the hero and the lonely ghost motifs. [9] It is not rare to find details of the deities personal life, family situation, and character mixed with the most fantastic kinds of miraculous events, together usually with the elements stressing the filial piety and loyalty of the subject. The close combination of the antithetical elements of familial renunciation and filial piety are striking.

An example of such a tale concerns Ma-tsu, patroness of shipping and fishermen, whose cult though relatively late, has spread widely from her native place in Meichou Island. There exist many stories about the origin of Ma-tsu. Most stress her great filial piety in helping her mother and in trying to save her father and brothers who were lost in a shipwreck. Because she could not save her father she vowed never to marry, so as to help her mother, and began to cultivate

her spirit.  She died at the age of 28 and later demonstrated efficacious miracles, particularly for fishermen.

Various stories stress the fact that the birth of Ma-tsu was
due to the divine intervention of Kwan-yin, and that Ma-tsu defeated
the enemy in war, and eventually ascended to heaven as an immortal;
when the news of her exploits reached the court after about 100 years,
she received an official title.  (Sokeirai: 273-275)

The outstanding element is the fact that she died without
marrying and childless, and hence was in face a "lonely ghost" at the
time she died, and that the villagers in the town where she lived
worshipped her (Ibid. 275).  Hence it is possible that the cult of
Ma-tsu began not as a cult to a national hero or to a renowned spiritual practitioner, but instead as the cult to a "ghost," and that the
legends about Ma-tsu represent a later "sanitized" version.

## The Genesis of Gods in Tanshui

The processes that have been detailed in the foregoing material can still be documented in Taiwan today.  Not only can many lesser
gods be shown to conform to the pattern of spirits without descendants,
but the major deities of the area as well follow this pattern, including Ma-tsu and Ch'ing-shui tsu-shih.  Moreover, if we include the
various Buddhas and Bodhisattvas as exemplars of the same tradition of
breaking the family tie, then we may say that most of the major deities
of the area conform.

To begin with, the <u>Yu-ying kung</u> spirits as a class belong to
this category, and represent the first stage in the process of the
genesis of gods.  These spirits which are by far the most numerous in
Taiwan are usually found housed in small shrines a few feet square, on
almost any street.

The Yu-ying kung cult centers around a person whose descendants are either unknown or absent.  Often these are bones which have
been accidently uncovered either by natural forces or by human agency.
Sometimes, however, they are the victims of warfare, drowning, or
violent death.  I am told that the basis of the cult is to find a piece
of bone and burn incense and paper money in front of it.  At first
there may be no shrine, no fixed celebration day, nor any organized
worshipping pattern.  Worshippers may come to worship on their own,
separately, perhaps at night.

In some cases the members of a neighborhood may combine to
erect a small shelter for the bone jar of the deceased.  This, for
example, was done with several abandoned jars full of bones that were
situated not far from my house.  Later people in the neighborhood even
erected a small shrine to house these bones.  Abandoned bones may be
called "unrelated ghosts" (wu yuan keui), or "unrelated Buddha," but
when they are enshrined they are generally known by the title Yu-ying
kung.  Frequently these names and titles include familial reference or
address terms such as "kung," which may be glossed as grandfather or
any friendly or respected person, "ma," mother as in "public mother"
(Ta-chung ma), "Po," paternal uncle as in "An-le po," etc.  However,
such terms do not usually indicate respect or love but rather fear.

(cf. Sokeirai: 90-91).

Fear is a strong motivating factor in early stages of the cult when the deceased person is still remembered and is being propitiated, and fame is important in the genetive stages of the cult as well as in its later development. Usually, however, the Yu-ying kung does not succeed in attracting a large following, no miracles are associated with its cult, and gradually it is forgotten, and the bone jar becomes one of thousands scattered throughout the countryside.

In fact, it must be the exceptional rarity that develops further, into a fully developed cult having a festival day, an organized following, a shrine, and perhaps a cult organizer to oversee the ritual events.

One such example was the case of the An-le po, a god whose shrine in Tanshui was at the end of the street on which I lived.

The An-le po was the spirit of a man who had died in the neighborhood about seventy-eight years ago. In addition to being without progeny, the man was poor, a condition frequently linked with chilelessness. In fact, we may say that poverty, childlessness and loneliness after death are all milestones on the same road. This beggar was much reviled during his life, I am told, and greatly feared after his death. So after he had passed away, there began a cult in his honor on his death anniversary which was intended to propitiate this potentially malevolent force. Some thirty years ago the present shrine was completed, and from that day on there grew a regular worship in his honor. Normally, this would have been performed on his birthday, but since this date was "unknown" the worshippers chose instead to celebrate the occasion each year in commemoration on the day that the shrine was finally completed. Today this god is considered as fearful and efficacious by many people in the four wards surrounding the shrine, and the number of worshippers has steadily increased. In order to support his worship an annual subscription is collected in the neighborhood based on a head tax of five NT per inhabitant. All households feel bound to pay this amount regardless of their feelings towards the spirit, by "following the custom of the neighborhood." The head of the household in which I lived, scoffed "why should I worship this An-le po, I had no connection with him when he was alive," but he contributed none the less. Most of the homes in the area sent representatives with offerings of food to the services. In addition, three operas were performed. Two were paid for by the inhabitants of the neighborhood, and the third was offered jointly by all those people who felt that their wishes had been answered by the deity.

During the afternoon in which these events were proceeding I witnessed an event take place which shed a light on the mechanisms by which such cults may become popularized. A small boy, the child of one of the ladies who came to worship, was struck by a motorcycle while crossing the street to go to the shrine. The motorcycle was not traveling fast and the child was not seriously injured, in fact he was only shaken up. But this fact was attributed to the miraculous power of the deity and in a few hours the tale of it had spread throughout the neighborhood. "What would have happened," I asked, "if the child had been seriously hurt or killed?" In that case, I was told, "the police would have come and the festival would have stopped."

This cult now attracts people from well beyond the limits of the neighborhood, and its god seems to possess all of the necessary factors for developing into a major deity in the area:  a reputation for efficacy and miracles, and a willing helper in the person of the temporary cult director (the former temple keeper of a temple in town).

Another example, though not from Tanshui, of the development of such a cult was told to me by a worshipper in a local temple.

Some years ago a dead body floated to the shore of the river at Erh Chung Pu and came to rest in some bamboo.  The body was buried by the police, but since the inhabitants of the place could not determine his identity they called him "Mister Bamboo Head."  Later people began to bring offerings to worship him, and eventually this became a regular occurrence on the first and fifteenth of every month, "because they believed that he would be less harmful if he had something to eat."  Some people came to petition him and got an efficacious reply. One worshipper had a child who was blinded by pustules in the eyes caused by an outbreak of measles.  She petitioned the deity after trying various kinds of medicines prescribed by doctors.  Through divination the spirit told her to mix water with incense ashes from his censer, and to pour this in the child's eyes.  She did so, and after a few days the disease disappeared.  After this the cult grew in size and reputation.

Although the Yu-ying kung worship today is usually centered around abandoned bones, this form of worship may have derived from the abandonment of corpses in olden days.

We have a rare description of the abandonment of corpses in the following report by a missionary in Tanshui.

"In 1878 a girl living not far from Tamsui wasted away
and died, a victim of consumption.  Someone in that neighborhood, more gifted than the rest, announced that a goddess was
there, and the wasted skeleton of the girl became immediately
famous.  She was given the name Sien-lu-niu ("Virgin Goddess"),
and a small temple was erected for her worship.  The body was
put into salt and water for some time, and then placed in a
sitting position in an armchair, with a red cloth around the
shoulders and a wedding-cap upon the head; and seen through
the glass, the black face, with the teeth exposed, looked
very much like an Egyptian mummy.  Mock money was burned and
incense-sticks laid in front.  Passers-by were told the story,
and as they are willing to worship anything supposed to have
power to help or harm, the worship of this new goddess began.
Before many weeks hundreds of sedan-chairs could be seen passing and repassing, bringing worshippers, especially women, to
this shrine.  Rich men sent presents to adorn the temple, and
all took up the cry of this new goddess.  But the devotees
were disappointed, for the divining-blocks gave no certain
answers; and while they might continue to reverence an un-
answering goddess whom their ancestors had worshipped before
them, they had not the same respect for a new candidate.

One woman who had heard the gospel several years before, while
we were preaching in the town of Kim-pau-li, was being carried
to worship at this temple; and when on a high narrow path,
through some accident she was tumbled down the bank in her
sedan-chair.  She returned home very much displeased with herself, and angry at those who introduced this new object of
worship.  Her confidence in the idol was all the more easily
shaken because of the secret working in her mind and heart
of the gospel heard years before.  Indeed, all attempts to
make the worship of this new goddess popular and universal
failed, and failed because 'the light of life was in the
field.'  A hundred years ago, however, she would soon have
had millions before her presenting their offerings and be-
seeching her favor."  (Mackay: 127-128).

Further evidence that today's gods may have been abandoned
corpses in the past is furnished by many cultic and mythic elements
surrounding the gods who are popular in Tanshui today.

One of the most striking examples, and one which lends further credence to the belief that ghosts eventually become worshipped
as gods, is the cult of Ta-shih yeh.

Ta-shih yeh, "The King of the Ghosts," is believed to be the
official who is in charge of all the hungry ghosts.  His cult occupies
an intermediate position between that of the ghosts and the gods.
Ta-shih yeh has attributes of both, and mediates between them by con-
trolling the ghosts for the deities.  This spirit is generally found
in conjunction with the Ma-tsu cult.  In Tanshui he was worshipped
during the seventh month ghost festival in the Ma-tsu temple.

This spirit has horns and a long tongue "to indicate that he
is ugly."  Even more interesting is the fact that he also carries the
name Chiao-mien ta-shih (Dried face official), which seems to indicate
that he too developed from what once was a withered corpse.

The symbol of the deity who is incorruptible after death is
found in a number of cult elements in the form of the black faced
deity.  Both the Ch'ing-shui and the Ma-tsu deities have black faces
and people attribute this to the great age of the statues and the number of worshippers who burn incense in front of the statue.  This
explanation, which seems reasonable on the surface, may not be the
real reason for the black faces of the deities.  I suggest an alternative story of the origins of the Ch'ing-shui tsu-shih which explains
the color of the deities' faces as well as revealing the origin of the
god.

In the first instance we have the account that the Tsu-shih
was a famous monk during the Sung Dynasty, and that by his practice
of meditation, he attained to Buddhahood, and hence became worshipped
as a Buddha.  This is the story which is often told by people associated with his cult.  However, there is little about the cult which
strikes the observer as Buddhist, and his status as a Buddha is hotly
contested by local Buddhists.

The second story about the Ch'ing-shui tsu-shih is what I

call the official temple story, for it is inscribed on a plaque in the Ch'ing-shui temple in Taipei's Wan hua district. Here he is cast in the role of a "hero."

"The patron saint of Ch'ing-shui yen, whose name was Ch'en chao-ying, was a native of Honan Province. He joined the Imperial army in 1127 A.D. when Sung kao-tsung, an Emporer of the Sung Dynasty, was on his expedition in the southern part of China, and distinguished himself as an able, patriotic soldier. After that he led a group of immigrants to Anchi in Fukien Province and took up his residence in the village of Ching-shui Yen in Pengnei.

Deploring the invasion by the Mongolians, he travelled around Fukien and Chekiang in the disguise of a Buddhist monk, secretly plotting against the invaders, but all of his efforts proved in vain in the long run. He then returned home and told his children and the villagers how deplorable it was that China had repeatedly suffered from the invasions of foreigners since the beginning of the Sung Dynasty, and exhorted them to exert themselves for the restoration of the Chinese race.

After his death he was deified and worshipped as the patron saint because of his loyalty to the Chinese race. The Temple dedicated to him has been called Ching-shui Yen Tsu-shih miao, or the temple of the patron saint of the Ching-shui Yen."

This story, which appears plausible on the surface, is probably a later, though perhaps still ancient, rationalization of a chain of events which were perhaps altogether different. If, however, he did have children it is unlikely that the cult would ever have begun. In all probability the story is a somewhat later development purporting to establish the origin of a deity which had already come into some prominence.

There is yet another story, exemplifying the third way in which men may become deified which, in addition, explains why the deity has a black face, a detail which is left out of the previous versions. This story, which was related to me on several different occasions by different informants, goes as follows:

"The Ch'ing-shui tsu-shih was actually a person called Ch'en P'u-tsu who was much disliked by his neighbors because of his ugly looks, so he left home and went to Ch'ing-shui cave in order to cultivate his mind. Since Ch'ing-shui cave was a very cold place, after he died, his body was not putrified or decayed, but turned black from the cold. People from the village of Hsiaoku in Anchi Prefecture of Fukien, found the body and began to worship it. Later a statue of the deity was brought to Taiwan."

This story explains all of the traits of the cult, the color of the face, and the reason for Buddhist clothes, as well as alluding to the fact that the worship began not because this person was a national hero, but because he was a homeless spirit feared and hated by his neighbors.

The theme of the preserved body is of great significance in understanding the different natures of the community god, the Buddha, and the ancestor.  In the case of the ancestor, as Ahern has pointed out, the preservation of the flesh on the bones of a corpse is looked at with particular horror by the descendants, for while it is thought to be good for the deceased, it is bad for the living survivors because the relinquishment of flesh is symbolic of the abdication of worldly powers (204-5).

Such a rationale, while of great significance in studying the affective economic and social ties within the family, is of course inoperative in the case of the community god.

In the case of the lonely ghost who becomes the deity, these ties are broken by virtue of the fact that the spirit has died without progeny, and thus ruptured the ties himself.  After death his body, if it does not decay, reveals its supernatural powers, its efficacy.  This body may be worshipped so long as it is still considered as a ghost, but due to the pollution of death, the corpse may not be put on the altar of the community temple because the distinction between life and death is most strongly marked within the community religion. [10]  This association of the god to the ghost must be broken, and the wooden statue of the god is substituted.

As for the immortal, he keeps his flesh body and lives in the world, as a sign of his victory over death.

I have attempted in the preceding examples to demonstrate that the main deities of the popular religion in the region have one common denominator; they are people who either left the home life or died without progeny.  If at some subsequent age they were made into heros or attributed with supernormal powers during their lifetimes, such attainments may belong to a later stage of the development of the deity.

We may pick up the subsequent stage in the canonization of these deities at a much later period during the final decades of the 19th century, at the time when their followers had brought them to Tanshui and had enshrined their statues in homes and temples.  At that time, in 1884, the French Navy had blockaded the ports of Keelung and Tanshui, and after launching a furious naval bombardment of the forts at Keelung, had captured that city and advanced towards Taipei. Hoping to make a pincer movement against the capital, the French decided to attack Tanshui as well, which they did after shelling the city and the Chinese fort at the mouth of the river.  Several units of marines were then landed to engage the native garrison; much to the surprise of everyone, not only did this attack fail, but the French fordes were repulsed with heavy losses.  (Garnot, Ch. I,II)

The local legends of the event present a more colorful account of the train of events:  The French attacked with 15 warships and bombarded the city with shells which, miraculously, failed to explode. The Chinese had only a single cannon, but miraculously two shells struck the French ships.  The French landed 2000 soldiers, but these were met and defeated by Chinese soldiers dressed in yellow.  People believed that these were transformation bodies of the Ch'ing tsu-shih, and said

that the credit for the victory was due to the gods, and not due to
the local militia.  Later the governor, Liu Ming-chuan, presented the
case to the Imperial court, and in return the Emperor presented three
plaques to the major deities of Tanshui:  The Kwan-yin at Lung-shan
Temple, the Ma-tsu, and the Ch'ing-shui tsu-shin.  At the same time
the "Misty Ocean City God" in Taipei was credited with helping to drive
the French out of that city, and he was granted the official title by
the court of "Awesome Efficacy Marquis" (Sokeirai: 318).  It was from
this time that his ascendancy began as City God of Taipei.  The plaques
which were given to the gods may be seen today hanging in their temples.

Soon thereafter the granting of titles by the court ceased.
But in the meantime Taiwan had been invaded by the Japanese, and
these gods continued to have a patriotic role to play in the lives of
the townsmen.  There are many stories told about the ways in which the
Ch'ing-shui tsu-shih made fun of the Japanese authorities.  During
World War II, while Taiwan was being bombed, several of the temples in
Tanshui were damaged by bombs, but we are told that miraculously nobody
was hurt.  The interior walls of the Ching-shui temple are scarred to
this day by shrapnel from an American bomb that fell in the courtyard.
If one looks closely at the large incense burners in this temple one
might remark that they are in the shape of large bombs.  Perhaps this
is the stuff of future legends.

During the war we are also told the Ma-tsu from the Kwantu
temple was efficacious in preventing American bombers from destroying
the large railway bridge across the Tanshui River, apparently witnesses
perceived among the bomb bursts the figure of Ma-tsu waving the bombs
away with a large fan.

Deities have also been effective in the post-war world; an
informant from a Buddhist temple tells us that once their temple was
occupied by large numbers of troops who would not move away.  One night
in his dreams the commander of the troops was told by a large red-faced
man to move out by a certain date; he readily complied.  The temple
staff claims that this was the efficacious response of Wei-t'o, the
guardian of Buddhist temples.

In summary, not everyone can become a god, and demonstrate
efficacy.  I have suggested that in the case of immortals and ancestors
this was prevented by the unlikelihood of reciprocal relations between
them and the worshippers.

The most likely candidates for the position of gods were the
hungry ghosts, who had to be propitiated and worshipped by the community as a whole in order to rid the community of malevolent influences.
Moreover, the ghosts, having no descendants of their own, might be
expected to lend a helping hand to those who worshipped them.

But the worship of ghosts in expectation of some return was
condemned both by the canons of confucian orthodoxy, and by the logical
segregation of life and death influences by the community as a whole.

As particular ghosts demonstrated their efficacy and were
elevated to the status of gods, it became necessary to conceal their

true origins. This was done eithey by myths in which they were cast in
the role of heros, and paragons of filial piety, or by the transformation of the cult within the arena of community practices, from the cult
of a dead person into that of a living god.

Some community gods were, as a result of their popularity
accepted into the official pantheon. On the other hand, many of the
gods in the official pantheon never became the objects of popular worship, because they were without this proven efficacy.


Footnotes

[1]   On Taiwan we have the case of Koxinga. Some of the Wang Yeh gods
      who seem to have specific Taiwanese roots were early officials
      who died fighting aboriginals or local bandits. (cf. Sokeirai:
      126)

[2]   Ancestor worship is only partly reciprocal. Descendants in
      theory are never supposed to be able to fully repay their debt
      to their ancestors.

[3]   A debt (or promise) to a god had to be paid back in full as soon
      as possible, generally within one calendar year. There is a
      saying in Taiwan, "You may owe a debt to ordinary people but you
      cannot owe a debt to a deity." So while the patterns of reci-
      procity between ancestors and descendants are focused on the long
      term, those between gods and men are temporary, and strictly
      reciprocal. If the deity does not grant your wish, or if mis-
      fortune strikes your family, all debts to the deity may be can-
      celled.

[4]   There are many differences between the community god and the
      Buddha figure. Buddha figures are not usually individualized
      statues with efficacious powers which move about patrolling an
      "area of control," like community gods do; as such they are poor
      symbols of the spatial community. This topic has been dealt with
      by the author in an unpublished paper entitled "Moving and Static
      Gods," delivered to the Anthropology Colloquium, Univ. of Pitts-
      burgh, June 1972.

[5]   A Taoist once remarked that Buddhist and Taoist cults were propa-
      gated differently: "The ordinary deities (shen) spread by pro-
      ducing miraculous effects, while the Buddhas are spread through
      proselytization."

[6]   For this reason I label them "community cults" in opposition to
      "family cults" which unite fellow agnates.

[7]   Because money has a purifying effect, it plays an important role
      in the purification of ghosts and their transformation into gods.

[8]   Adoption of worshippers by the deities is a very prevalent cus-
      tom in Taiwan even today, and is believed to create a particu-
      larly efficacious link between the deity and the child. This link
      is, however, a temporary one, as it is broken when the child
      attains maturity and becomes a full fledged member of his own
      lineage, usually at about the age of 16.

[9]   Although they are usually distinct, in people's minds the two

extremes of 'lonely ghost' and 'hero-god' sometimes have struck
a happy medium of acceptability in the figure of the local hero
who dies defending the realm against internal and foreign
enemies, often at the cost of extinguishing his own family line.

[10]  Corpses and bones are considered to be particularly polluting to
the purity of the "community temple" as is any contact with death.
I suspect that this fact derives in part at least from an unconscious attempt to deny the very origin of the community god.  In
contrast, Buddhist bone temples are not thus jeopardized; which
underlines again the fundamental difference between the Buddha
and the community god.



Bibliography

Ahern, Emily M., The Cult of the Dead in a Chinese Village (Stanford:
    Stanford University Press, 1973).

Eberhard, Wolfram, Studies in Chinese Folklore and Related Essays
    (The Hague:  Mouton, 1970).

Feng-shen pang; Feng-shen yen-i, Author Unknown, Partial Translation,
    W. Grube Feng-shen yen-i, die Metamorphoses der Götter (Leiden:
    1912).

Garnot, Captain, L'éxpedition Française de Formose, 1884-1885
    (Paris:  C. Delagrave, 1894).

Lin  Heng-tao, "Religious classification of the enshrined deities,"
    T.W.W.H., Vol. 13, Dec. 1962, pp. 100-110 (In Chinese).

Mackay, George Leslie, D.D.  From Far Formosa, Ed. by Rev. J. A.
    Macdonald (New York:  H. Revell Co., 1896).

Shryock, J. K., The Temples of Anking and their Cults (Paris:  Geuthner,
    1931).

Sokeirai (Tseng Ching-lai), The Religious and Debased Superstitions of
    Taiwan (Taihoku: 1938) (In Japanese).

THE FANTASTIC AND THE SACRED IN THE WRITINGS OF MIRCEA ELIADE

Mac Linscott Ricketts

Louisburg College

In the introduction to his book, The Sacred and the Profane, Mircea Eliade says much about the "sacred" and the experience of the "sacred" without ever clearly defining what he means by this term. He makes reference to Rudolf Otto's Das Heilige without criticism, seemingly accepting Otto's "idea of the holy" as his starting point, but rather than dealing with religious experience as such, Eliade attempts in this book to eludidate the "modalities of the sacred," and to show the difference between religious man who wants to live "in the sacred" and the non-religious or modern man who chooses to live in a desacralized world.

The sacred and the profane, Eliade says further (p. 14), are "two modes of being in the world, two existential situations assumed by man in the course of his history." In this statement, "sacred" and "profane" are being used to define opposite types of life, contrasting the response of man to what Eliade calls the hierophany, the self-manifestation of the sacred, with the life-form of the man who recognizes no such experience. The following statement comes closer to being a definition of the term: ". . . For primitives as for the man of all premodern societies, the sacred is equiva- lent to a power, and in the last analysis, to reality. The sacred is saturated with being." (p. 12) The term "sacred," then, refers to the Ultimately Real. Like Otto, Eliade calls the sacred the ganze andere (ibid).

These statements clarify matters somewhat, but we are still left to wonder precisely what Eliade conceives the sacred to be. Is the sacred simply a convenient catch-all term for mankind's various ideas of God, Brahman, the Tao, etc.? Does the term correspond to something metaphysically real, or does it designate men's illusions of reality? Eliade does not attempt to deal with metaphysical questions in his writing on the history of religions, apparently because he does not consider this an appropriate activity for an historian of religions as such. However, in his more personal writings -- his autobiography, protions of his Journal which he has released, and in his fiction -- Eliade leave no doubt that he personally believes in the reality of that which manifests itself to man as the supernatural and transhistorical.

Most historians of religion are acquainted with only one side of Eliade's complex literary production. In addition to his numerous books and articles on the history of religions, Eliade has written and continues to write fiction in his native Romanian: novels, short stories, and plays. Since adolescence he has kept a journal or diary almost continuously, and parts of this have been published. The first volume of an autobiography, ending with his departure for India in 1929, exists in Romanian, and other chapters have been written. A small part of these have been translated and published in French, German, or English (see bibliography), but the majority have not. When these become accessible to American readers, a whole new phase of "Eliade studies" will open. It is hoped that it will be possible to publish these soon.

The central idea which runs through all of these, like a crimson thread, is the paradox of the hierophany, or as Eliade has also called it, the "dialectic of camouflage,"[1] that is, "the problem of the unrecognizablilty of miracle, the fact that the intervention of the sacred into the world is always camouflaged in a series of 'historical forms,' of manifestations which do not apparently differ in any way from millions of cosmic or historical forms."[2]

In his autobiography[3] Eliade describes an early childhood experience which can only be called "mystical." One summer's afternoon when he was about four years of age, the rest of the household was napping. Little Mircea gained entry into the large formal living room of the old mansion in Bucharest in which they were living, a room ordinarily kept closed. Something about the greenish light of the room, caused by the sunlight's being filtered through green curtains, produced an indescribable sensation of another world. Eliade reflects on the experience:

"Had I been able to use adult vocabulary, I might have said that I had discovered a mystery. . . I could later evoke at will this green fairyland. When I did so, I would remain motionless, almost not daring to breathe,, and I would rediscover that blessedness (_beatitudinea_) all over again. I would relive with the same intensity the moment when I had stumbled into that paradise of incomparable light. I practiced for many years this exercise of recapturing the epiphanic moment, and I would always rediscover the same plenitude. I would let myself slip into it as into a fragment of time devoid of duration. . ."

Slightly modified, this highly impressive event finds a place in Eliade's greatest novel, _Noapte de Sanziene_, as an episode in the life of the principal character, Ştefan Viziru.

As a child of about nine during the German occupation of Bucharest during the First World War, Eliade discovered he could create an army of his own in his imagination. Lying half-asleep on his bed, he visualized involuntarily a cornfield near the city in which Romanian troops were hiding. The more he dwelt on the image in his reveries each day, the larger the army grew. It found a hidden arsenal, engaged in battles with the Germans, and won victories. As Eliade describes the experience: "I did not, in fact, imagine it -- rather, I _saw_ what was happening on a interior movie screen" (p. 34). He tried to write down this story which was "revealing itself" to him, but without success. When he began writing, the vision vanished. Later, however, he would be more successful in putting his imaginary narratives onto paper.

Through these and similar experiences, Eliade discovered "other worlds," other temporal rhythms, other modes of existing in the world. Without going out of the historical world physically, he yet found it possible to emerge from it mentally. The experience of the creative artist is thus, structurally, like that of the religious man: he experiences another world along side his own, which for him is as real or _more_ _real_ than that of the everyday world.

From his early adolescence Eliade has been a prolific writer, and his writings have been always of both fictional and non-fictional types. In the spring of the year when he was thirteen, he produced for an assignment in his Romanian class in the _liceu_ a fantasy on the coming of spring, which he first "visualized" as he had the story of his secret army. He discovered then that he could write down such experiences "after this reverie had attained an intensity and beautitude that was hard to bear" (p. 58). As a result, he produced in the ensuing months a whole notebook full of stories, most of them fantasies.[4] But along side this kind of creative writing, Eliade began at the same time to keep notebooks on scientific subjects: things he was reading or biological researches he was carrying on.[5]

His first published article was entitled, "The Enemy of the Silkworm," a little "scientific" essay which appeared in the autumn of 1920 in _Ziarul Ştiinţelor Populare_ (The Paper of Popular Sciences) when the writer was only thirteen. That winter he submitted to the same publication a prize-winning composition entitled, "How I Discovered the Philosopher's Stone," a fantasy based on an alchemical theme.[6] The editors were so impressed that from this date he was allowed to become a regular

contributor, writing a column called "Entomological Conversations," which continued
for several years.  It was about this same time, Eliade recalls, that he began to
keep a journal.[7]

        After these excursions into the realms of the fantastic, Eliade seems
largely to have abandoned this literary  genre for the next decade and a half, until
the  the writing of Domnişoara Christina (1936) and Şarpele (1937).   During this time
he was engaged first in studies of philosophy and religion (his licentiate thesis was
in the field of the Italian Renaissance and his doctoral dissertation on yoga), and
later in teaching at the Universtiy of Bucharest.  While still in the liceu he wrote
a highly autobiographical novel in which he strove for authenticity, and followed it
with another in university days on the life of the college student.  (These were never
published.)  Several novels of a semi-autobiographical nature, plus others on more
imaginative themes date from the early 1930's.  He was also writing regularly for a
a religious newspaper, Cuvântul (The Word), for most of these years.  In 1932 Eliade
published a small book of philosophical musings which he had been writing for about
four years, Soliloquii, in which  he   shows himself already beginning to be concerned
with the problem of the camouflage of the sacred in the profane, as he later states.[8]

        Domnişoara Christina is a story of a ghost or vampire who cannot bear to
give up the desires and longings for love which were proper to her condition before
her untimely death as a young woman.  Consequently, she tries to make love to young
men, partly through the person of her pre-pubescent neice.  Eliade was pleased that
in this novel he was able to create an atmosphere of fantasy and horror without employ-
ing typical folkloric motifs all to commonly used by Romanian writers.[9]

        He returned to fantasy again the next year with the short novel, Şarpele
(The Snake).  Written under the pressure of a heavy work schedule and in great haste
in the wee hours of the morning (a chapter a night over a two-week period, without
opportunity to reread what he had written), Eliade confesses that he was astonished
when the galley-proofs arrived and he was able to read the book as a whole  -- it had
a stylistic unity he had rarely been able to achieve before.[10]   This novel, which
has been published in a German translation as well as in the Romanian, has to do with
party of quite ordinary people who go on an overnight outing to a monastery park where
they encounter a mysterious young man, Andronic.  The influence of Andronic is such
as to project the others, individually and collectively, into "another world" --
though physically they remain at the monastery.  Unlike the situation in Domnişoara
Christina, however, in Şarpele the fantastic world does not burst in upon this one
as an utterly foreign intrusion, but it unfolds itself gradually and without discon-
tinuity.  As Eliade says:

    ". . . The 'fantastic' world in which, thanks to Andronic, they find themselves
    after midnight, is the same as the everyday one -- with the single difference
    that it discloses now an added dimension, inaccessible to profane existence.
    It is as if the everyday world camouflages a secret dimension which, once man
    knows it, reveals to him simultaneously the profound significance of the
    Cosmos and his authentic mode of being: a mode of perfect, blissful spontaniety,
    but which is neither irresponsible animal existence nor angelic beautitude.

    "Without knowing it and without intending it, I succeeded in 'showing' in
    Şarpele something which I developed later in my works of philosophy and history
    of religions, namely that, apparently the 'sacred' is not different from the
    'profane' and that the 'fantastic' is camouflaged in the 'real,' that the world
    is what it shows itself to be and at the same time is a cipher. . . In a
    certain sense one could say that this theme constitutes the key to all my
    mature works."[11]

It should be noticed how Eliade in the above quotation contrasts the
fantastic with the real in a way exactly parallel to the contrast between the sacred
and the profane.  That is, the fantastic (in literature, at least) stands in the
same dialectical relationship to the "real world" as does the sacred to the profane
world.  Indeed, Eliade can speak of "profane existence" as an alternative term for
the opposite of the fantastic.  Does this mean that the fantastic and the sacred are
to be identified as two aspects of the same reality?  I believe that for Eliade this
is .the case.

Speaking of Şarpele in another place,[12]  Eliade states that one thing which
the writing of that book taught him was that "the free act of literary creation can
. . . reveal certain theoretical meanings.  Indeed, only after I reread Şarpele as a
whole did I realize that in this book I had resolved without knowing it a problem
which had preoccupied me long before . . . and which I had expounded somewhat system-
atically only in Traite (= Patterns in Comparative Religion), namely, the problem of
the unrecognizability of miracle, the fact that the intervention of the sacred into
the world is always camouflaged in a series of 'historical forms.'"  In this quotation,
already cited in part before, it is plain that Eliade sees the sacred, the miraculous,
and the fantastic  as so many aspects of the same thing -- something which we may
designate as "the supernatural."

After Şarpele Eliade published two short stories which have been translated
into English and published under the title, Two Tales of the Occult.  One story, "The
Secret of Dr. Honigberger," is set in Bucharest but has to do with magical powers
supposedly attainable through the practice of yoga.  The other, "Nights at Serampore,"
takes place in and around Calcutta and centers upon the experience of three Europeans
who seem to have been projected back in time 150 years due to the influence of a
practitioner of tantric yoga.  Both tales allow Eliade to display his knowledge of
yoga and while their purpose seems primarily to entertain, they do present yoga as a
means of attaining mastry over time and space.

Following the end of the Second World War Eliade settled in Paris and wrote
in French those books on the history of religions and philosophy of culture which made
him world-famous.  Meanwhile, however, and unknown to all but a few friends, Eliade
was composing fiction in his mother-tongue.  Between 1945 and 1974 Eliade has written
some fourteen short stories, one play, and one enormous novel.  Most of these were
published originally in Romanian exile publications, and two collections
of stories were published in book form.  The novel, Noapte de Sânziene (Night of St.
John) was first published in French (Forêt Interdite), but subsequently appeared in
Romanian.  Almost all of these writings contain fantasy to some degree.

Three of these stories are available in English: "A Great Man,"  Twelve
Thousand Head of Cattle," and "With the Gypsy Girls."  (See bibliography.)  In the
first, a man suddenly becomes afflicted with "macanthropy" and rapidly outgrows the
human condition, becoming in effect a mahāpuruşa.  When he escapes the city, reaches
the mountains, and reintegrates himself in nature, he cries, "It is good!"  A business-
man in  "Twelve-Thousand Head of Cattle" experiences a sudden exit from historical
time in midday, being projected back into the time of an air raid some forty days
previous.  The novella, "With the Gypsy Girls," is a masterpiece of fantasy.  Gavrilescu, the middle-aged piano teacher, a failure in life, steps across the threshold of
the gypsy girls' place somewhere in Bucharest, and enters another world of space and
time.

There is not space here to say more than a few words about the fantastic elements
in Eliade's other fictional writings which await publication in English.  "Ghictor în
pietre" (The Man Who Could Read Stones; 1959) is very difficult to fathom, but apparent-

ly it presents the case of a man who, like Gavrilescu, falls into another world
existing parallel to that of every day, but one in which he also has been living
without knowing it. "O fotografie vechi de 14 ani" (A Photograph Fourteen Years
Old; 1959), Eliade's only story set in America, revolves around the miraculous
cure of an asmatic woman through the faith of her husband in a "faith healer" who
is really a fraud. She is cured at a distance, the preacher having nothing but an
old photo of the woman to look at, and she not only loses her asthma but also becomes
once again as young as she was in the picture.

Podul (The Bridge, 1964) consists of a lengthy conversation among four
passengers in a train compartment. The fantastic enters the story at the end when
one of the men steps off the train just after it has crossed a bridge, and we are
given to understand that for him the crossing of the bridge was his death.

Pe strada Mântuleasa (On Mântuleasa Street; 1955, 1967), a long and complex
work, presents " the encounter of two different, antagonistic, and yet finally
identical mythological worlds;"[13] that is, the fantastic world of the old school
teacher and that of his interrogators, the Communist bureaucracy of post-war Bucharest.
"In the frustrating process of interrogation the two worlds gradually impinge and
merge, and the bureaucratic world begins to function fantastically."[14]

"Ivan" (1967) is a tale about a young Romanian army officer and two of his
men, the only survivors of a platoon on the Russian front, who come upon a dying
Russian soldier as they are trying to find their way back to their unit through the
Ukrainian cornfields. It is a marvelous study in the shifting back and forth between
fantasy and reality -- only we are never quite sure which is which!

"În curte la dionis" (In the Court of Dionysos; 1968) continues the story of
a couple, Adrian and Leana, introduced in "Mântuleasa." The plot is quite obscure, and
it is difficult to say where simple mystery ends and true fantasy begins.

In "Uniforme de General" (1971) fantasy appears in the reveries of Ieronim,
the writer and producer of experimental plays, and at the end in what is apparently
the death of Antim, Ieronim's uncle, a master cellist, when his "true love" comes for
him as his angel of death. To a certain extent Antim's life, like that of Adrian in
"Dionis", is a reinactment of myth, since he has lived his life under the shadow of a
story he read in childhood.

In his most recent short story, "Incognito in Buchenwald" (1974), Ieronim
appears again, along with some characters from "Mântuleasa" and "Dionis." At the end
of the story, young Ieronim and the ageless Marina, a semi-fantastic figure, witness
a mystic transformation of Bucharest: as the old family mansion is being demolished
by workmen, through the dust they see the city transformed into a gleaming "new
Jerusalem" as it were.

Two other short stories, "Şanţurile" (The trenches, 1963) and "Adio!"
(Goodbye! 1964) contain only negligible fantastic elements.

The play, "Coloana nesfârşită" (The Endless Column, 1969) is about an historical personage, the Romanian sculptor Constantin Brâncuşi who flourished during
the first half of the present century. Nevertheless, the play is virtually a fantasy,
the only other character of significance being the scultpor's "anima," personfied as
"the Girl." Here again, as in "Uniforme," the play ends in a supernatural "translation" or death scene.

The great novel, Noapte de Sânziene, unfolds under the shadow of a fantastic
automobile which the hero, Ştefan, somehow knows belongs to his mysterious sweetheart

Ileana, and which will disappear on the Night of St. John (Midsummer's Night).  In
addition to this supernatural theme, the very love which Ştefan and Ileana have for
each other is a transcendent thing which can only be realized after death.  Moreover,
Ştefan's hyper-sensitivity to "signs" -- to secret meanings in seemingly ordinary
events and persons -- is a continuing fantastic element throughout the story.  (There
is much, much more in this book, but here is not the place to discuss it.)

     In addition to the fantastic elements which I have here sought to identify,
Eliade uses another technique in his fiction which has the effect of heightening the
"unreal" atmosphere of the narratives, and that is _mystery_.  Eliade states that the
"two tales of the occult" are written in the genre of "mystery stories,"[15]  but in
case of the other stories which are not construed in this form, Eliade leaves many
things obscure and unexplained until the end -- and sometimes even then he does not
completely enlighten the reader.  We cannot, of course, expect an explanation of
fantastic events -- if they were explained they would no longer be fantastic! -- but
in numbers of stories, especially the more recent ones, we are left puzzling about
events which are _not_ evidently intended to be fantastic.

     The most "mystifying" of the novellas probably is "In curte dionis," mentioned
briefly above.  The problem in making sense of this story hinges partly on Eliade's
failure to clarify the situation in the "real life" of the main characters -- it is all
very mysterious!  Eliade is aware of the difficulties he has created.  In his journal
for 16 June, 1968, after just having written the story, he asks himself who will
understand it, and _how_ _much_ will be understood?  Apparently Adrian, a victim of amnesia,
has wandered into another world, a kind of Hades ( a hotel with a flaming red carpet)
and from it Leana, in an inversion of the Orpheus-Eurydice myth, comes to resuce him.
How the amnesia began is alluded to briefly at the end of the story, but Eliade explains
these things only in his journal.  Yet, even for Eliade, it seems, there are mysteries
in the story.  Although he wrote it, he does not fully understand it:

     "But so many other things remain to be understood:  I still don't know
     _who_ Adrian is (Leana tells him that 'if he would show himself now' he would
     be understood). . .  Leana calls him 'Your Highness.'  Why?  Only because he
     is 'Prince of Poets' or because she loves him?"[16]

     These enigmatic remarks of Eliade's are highly significant.  They show us
that for him now, as when he was a child, the process of literary creation is somewhat involuntary, that he "sees" his stories and does not himself know all that his
characters mean.  Thus the process of the creation of fiction is itself evidence of
the existence of an irrational, transcendent realm of the mind, one with laws of its
own, out of which whole universes can be produced.

     There are unresolved mysteries also in the great novel.  We never learn,
for instance, how Vădastra survived the air raid or how he lived during the next
several years.  We are never told about Ştefan's involvement in political intrigue,
or what documents he took with him when he defected.  In "Podul" three of the men
involved in the conversation on the train talk about persons and events which remain
enigmas for the reader, simply because Eliade does not give us enough information
for us to make sense of them.  Likewise we are left puzzling at the end of "Şanţurile"
as to who fired the machine gun from the church belfry -- or is this an element of
fantasy?

     The device of leaving some essential piece of information undisclosed is
nothing new for Eliade.  In his autobiography he makes this remark about his early
story, "How I Discovered the Philosopher's Stone:"  "It began something like this:
I am in the lab and for some reason I have fallen asleep (but the reader would not

know this because I did not tell him).[17]

While one may complain now and then that Eliade has made his narratives
a bit too obscure, the overall effect of withholding  information is to intensify
the mystery, to get the reader involved in the fictional world or worlds of the
author's creation.  Mystery as well as fantasy are employed with great artistry by
our author.

And it is clear that what Eliade intends by his fiction is to "create new
worlds" into which the reader will allow himself to enter.  Being caught up in these
narratives, the reader is to become then open to the "message" which the stories are
intended to convey.

Writing about "La ţigănci" in his journal for 5 March, 1968 Eliade states:

". . . This story does not 'symbolize' anything; that is, it does not
transform immediate reality into a cipher.  The novella <u>founds</u> a world, a
Universe independent of the geography and sociology of Bucharest in the years
1930-40. . . It is a presentation of a new, original Universe with its own
laws -- and this presentation constitutes an <u>act of creation</u> -- not only in
the aesthetic sense of that term.  By penetrating this Universe, learning to
to know it, and relishing it, something <u>is revealed</u> to you.  The problem it
poses for the critics is not how to decipher the 'symbolism' of the story, but,
admitting that the story has 'enchanted' me and <u>convinced</u> me, how to interpret
the <u>message</u> which its reality conceals (more precisely, that new species of
reality which discoloses itself to me as I read the 'adventures' of Gavrilescu."[18]

In a further reflection on "La ţigănci" dated 10 March, 1968 Eliade
continues:

"Such literature founds its own Universe; just as a myth discloses to us
the foundation of the World, of modes of being (animals, plants, man, etc.),
of institutions, manners of behavior, etc.  In this sense it is possible to
speak about the prolongation of myth in literature, not only because certain
mythological structures and Figures are rediscovered in the imaginary universes of literature, but especially because in both instances it is a matter of
a 'creation' (='revelation') of a world parallel to the everyday Universe in
which we move.  'La ţigănci,' like a Polynesian or North American Indian myth
<u>is</u>, and <u>is not</u>, a 'real world' -- a world, that is, in which the ordinary man
lives or can live.  But just as in myth, 'La ţigănci' (and other novellas of
this sort) reveal unsuspected significances and <u>give</u> <u>meaning</u> to 'everyday life.'"

From these remarks I believe we should conclude that Eliade sees his literary
work as a kind of modern "myth-making."  He scorns styles of fiction writing which are
devoid of plot: instead, he believes the <u>story</u> is now, as in all times past, the best
verbal form for conveying messages.[19]  And it becomes increasingly clear as one reads
Eliade's literary works of the past twenty years, especially, that he has a message
which he wants to put across to the world.  There is not space here to develop this
point, but Eliade's message in briefest form concerns the reality of the transhistorical,
supernatural, or sacred realm.  As many of his characters say, "An exit exists!"
Freedom is possible -- freedom from time, history, and mortality, man's mode of being
in the world.  Since the sacred is always concealed within the profane, Eliade will
not proclaim his message in a direct and obvious way; rather he proclaims it in his
"literary mythology" and he writes about it objectively and "scientifically" in his
books on the history of religions.

Ieronim, the experimental play-maker in Eliade's two most recent short stories

seems to be a character close to Eliade's heart.  In "Uniforme de General" Ieronim
is entrusted with a secret, whispered to him by his dying aunt, the <u>Generăleasa</u>.
Other members of the family try for years to pry it our of him, but he says he has
promised to tell it to no one but his son when he shall reach the age of 18.  (However,
Ieronim is not married and has no son.)  When one elderly cousin on his death bed
begs Ieronim to reveal to him what the <u>Generăleasa</u> told him, he refuses, but adds:

> "But Luchian, . . . ever since that night when the <u>Generăleasa</u> called
> me to her bedside, I have done nothing else except talk about those things
> which which she confided in me!  But because I swore, I cannot speak them
> in the way they were told me by the tongue of the dying -- yet I reveal
> them in parables, in anecdotes, and images.  Ever since the <u>Generăleasa</u>
> died, I have done nothing else -- <u>I can do nothing else</u> -- except tell you,
> but obscurely, as in an old mirror. . . -- I can do nothing else but speak
> in images and parables about the secret which has been entrusted to me."[20]

This, I believe, is Eliade himself speaking, telling us his purpose, what
he has been trying to do for many years, to awaken us to the Truth which he has seen.
But the Truth cannot be spoken openly; it must be couched in images and parables,
because <u>thus the sacred always shows itself</u>, in and through the common forms of this
world.

"The unrecognizability of the sacred," the "dialectics of camouflage" --
it is this which unifies the diverse works of Mircea Eliade.  The one word <u>hier-
ophany</u> says it all: the self-revelation of the sacred, the veiled appearance in
our world of that which comes from beyond.


## NOTES

1.  <u>Two Tales of the Occult</u>, Introduction, p. x.

2.  "Fragment Autobiografic,"p. 10.

3.  <u>Amintiri</u>, p. 9.

4.  Later, when the notebook had long since perished with all other papers left
    behind in Romania, Eliade was to regret deeply that he could recall only
    fragments of these early works of imagination.  ("Carnet de vară,"p. 29.)

5.  <u>Amintiri</u>, pp. 59-60.

6.  <u>Ibid</u>., pp. 63-64.

7.  <u>Ibid</u>., p. 72.

8.  "Fragment Autobiografic," p. 10.  For example:  "Concerning the 'unseen God.'
    Jesus said, No one has seen him.  It is not a matter of his invisibility, but
    of his <u>unrecognizibility</u>."  (<u>Soliloquii</u>, p. 61.)

9.  "Bucureşti, 1937," pp. 58-59.

10.  <u>Ibid</u>., p. 63.

11.  <u>Ibid</u>., p. 64.

12.  "Fragment Autobiografic," p. 10.

13.  <u>Two Tales of the Occult</u>, Introduction, pp. xi-xii.

14.  <u>Ibid</u>., p. xii.

15. <u>Ibid</u>, p. ix.

16. Journal for 16 June, 1968.

17. <u>Amintiri</u>, p. 64.

18. Journal for 5 March, 1968;  cf. also Intorduction to <u>Two Tales of the Occult</u>, p. xii.

19. "Carnet de vară," pp. 27-28.

20. "Uniforme de General," typescript, p. 56.


BIBLIOGRAPHY

<u>Autobiographical Materials.</u>

"Fragment Autobiografic," <u>Caiete de Dor</u>, No. 7 (July, 1953).

"Carnet de vară," <u>Caiete de Dor</u>, No. 13 (June, 1960).  Journal for summer of 1958, largely reproduced in <u>Fragments d'un Journal</u>.

<u>Amintiri (I, Mansarda</u>), Madrid, Destin, 1966.

"Bucureşti, 1937," <u>Fiinta Romanească</u>, No. 5, 1966.

<u>Fragments d'un Journal</u>, trans. by Luc Badesco; Paris, Gallimard, 1973.  (In French.)

<u>Pe strada Mantuleasa,</u>  Caietele Inorgului.


<u>Fiction.</u>

<u>Noapte de Sânziene</u> (two volumes), Paris; Ion Cuşa, 1971.  (French translation, <u>Forêt Interdite</u>, tr. by Alain Guillermou,  Paris; Gallimard, 1955.)

<u>Nuvele</u>,  Madrid: Destin, 1963.  (A collection of short stories.)

<u>La ţigănci şi alte povestiri</u>,  Bucureşti, Editura pentru litertatură, 1969.  (Collection of short stories and novellas, including Domnişoara Christina  and Şarpele, as well as more recent ones.)  Contains an excellent introductory essay on "Dialectica fantasticul" (The Dialectic of the Fantastic) by Sorin Alexandrescu.

"Ivan",  <u>Destin</u>.

"Şanţurile," <u>Revista Scriitorilor Român</u>, No. 2, Munich: 1963.

<u>Coloana nesfârşită</u>,  Munich: Revista Scriitorilor Român, 1970.

"In curte la dionis,"  Uniforme de General", and "Incognito in Buchenwald,"  exist only in unpublished manuscripts.

<u>English Translations Published.</u>

<u>Fantastic Tales</u>, translated by Eric Tappe,  London: Dillon's, 1969.

<u>Two Tales of the Occult</u>, translated by William Ames Coates, New York: Herder and Herder, 1970.

"With the Gypsy Girls," translated by William Ames Coates,  <u>Denver Review</u>, 1973.

________________  ________________

<u>Soliloquii</u>,  Bucureşti:  Colectia carte cu semne, 1932.

WARRIORS: THE ORIGINATORS OF THE
MORAL CODE IN ANCIENT INDIA

by

Mary Carroll Smith

University of North Carolina, Chapel Hill

Morality and the practice of a good life is considered the domain of religion. The Sanskrit word for religion is <u>dharma</u>, but many scholars translate <u>dharma</u> as "duty," "law," or "right conduct," and the Indian translators include a notion of "the customary observances of caste."[1] The use of the notion of <u>dharma</u> in the epic <u>Mahābhārata</u> seems to be centered around the eldest Pāṇḍava brother, Yudhiṣṭhira, who has the epithet "King of Dharma." Thus in the <u>Śanti Parvan</u> which is called the book of the Dharma we hear:

> O Yudhisthira, always seek the companionship of Brahmins in
> all your acts. Brahmins constitute the great source of benefit
> both in this world and the next. They are teachers of duty and
> morality. They are always grateful. O powerful one, if they
> are worshipped, they are sure to do you good. Therefore, O King,
> you should always worship them. You will then, O King, duly
> obtain kingdom, great good, fame, achievements and progeny in
> their proper order.[2] (Mbh. 12.136.107f)

Although morality is a set of ideas for evaluating human acts, it has focus on action rather than on thought. In most societies moral life means a prescribed set of customs which regulate relationships and modes of behavior. The process of philosophical speculation on customs or behavior can be shown to be a late development in the history of a tribe or nation. India's sacred texts yield evidence that the origin and development of standards of morality resided in the <u>Kṣatriya</u> or the warrior caste. The <u>Ṛg Veda</u> and the <u>Mahābhārata</u> furnish proof that the priests were subject to the warriors for life and property. Yet in the last line quoted from the passage above, it is evident that at some one point a reversal of power took place. Since the commentaries and the oral formulaic codes and lists of good and bad behavior, such as found in the <u>Śanti Parvan</u> and the <u>Laws of Manu</u>, were compiled and developed by the Brahmins, it is natural to think of the priests as the originators of morality codes. By scientific study from a metrical, linguistic and narrative frame, it has become evident that the priests adopted warrior codes and thereby effected part of a shift of power and prestige which has remained with the Brahmin caste in India up to the present.

The great epic of India yields a hidden text of identifiable verses which appear to relate to the Vedic period. In this corpus of verses the warriors are in control. Priests are not involved in anything more than ceremonial action, and when they are mentioned as advisors to the king there is evidence of textual explication or emendation. The scope of the warriors is in full view. They are lords over land and life. Marriage, truth-swearing and revenge are their personal and proper domain while the Fire and attachment to the house or family of a warrior-king are the domain of the priests. The warriors steal brides and then fight off her pursuing relations if they escape then a tribal

-57-

alliance or marriage takes place.  Warriors gamble or fight because
they have "sworn an oath that they will never refuse a challenge."  If
they are wronged they gather their allies and wage war.  They view the
world with a drawn bow.  They never waste words.
     The text of the <u>Mahābhārata</u> which passed into manuscript form
has been the greatest determent to the study of the warrior caste. The
problems of considering the manuscript as a whole is best illustrated
by E.W. Hopkins' dilemma about morality:
> Let us reflect upon the fact, evident to anyone that has
> traced the lines of growth in Hindu civilization, that, as
> religion descended, morality ascended; that the later
> religious feeling was less simple and less pure than the
> earlier, but the later morality was higher and stricter
> than that of a former age; or that, at least, the didactic
> morality as last inculcated was superior to that recognized
> at first.  Consider how penetrated is the Epic by this later
> morality; how ethical need imposes long sermons on us (not
> religious) at every turn; how it has added chapter after chapter
> at variance with earlier feeling and custom; how it everywhere
> teaches abhorrence of wrong acts from a point of view often
> of sternest right; how it condemns the barbarities of an
> early uncivilized community; how it has composed a formal
> 'code of fighting' that inculcates law more humane than was
> possibly consistent with the practices of the older times
> commemorated by the first form of the poem — is it not
> reasonable to suppose that those same priests who framed the
> fighting code and endeavored to implant in their brutal
> warrior-kings a moral, not to say a chivalrous sentiment,
> might have been swayed by two opposing desires in handing
> down their national Epic?[3]

Hopkins never raises the question that a national Epic is the concern of
priests not kings.  More modern scholars have agreed that the text does
embody a Brahmin recension but until the computer was utilized for study
and sorting, there was no accurate way of separating the Brahmanic over-
lay.[4]  Since the nature of an oral tradition is just recently being made
the object of study, and since the great epic of India contains the mark
of at least two traditions that were sealed in different metre, the study
of the warriors is dependent on notions of oral text preservation and
transmission.[4]  There can be no doubt that the role of preserving and
transmitting texts belonged to the priest.

     Through the use of a computer for metrical scansion and sorting
I have been able to isolate a text of irregular 44 syllable verses called
<u>triṣṭubh</u>.  These verses which are largely dialogue contain a coherent
narrative pattern.  It is from this text of 8000 lines that I have been
able to study the Indian epic hero and his morality code.  The irregular
verses have points of correspondence with some Vedic situations, one of
which is the use of the term <u>vipra</u> rather than <u>brahman</u> for priest.  The
word <u>vipra</u> as it is used of the poet-priests in the Ṛg Veda may best be
translated as "Shaman".  Because the priests are almost invisible in the
8000 line text of irregular triṣṭubh verses in the <u>Mahābhārata</u> it is
worth looking at the priests of the Vasiṣṭha line in the Seventh Maṇḍala
of the Ṛg Veda.  Almost all of the hymns in this Maṇḍala are in the
triṣṭubh metre.

     The creation of "power songs" called <u>brahmāni</u> is the chief
concern of the poet-priests (<u>vipra</u>).  Through the use of his "power song"

the warrior-king is victorious. There is a clear division of labor; no
fighting priests or singing kings.  That the priest's song is connected
to the Soma cult is certain, but the exact relation of the hymns to the
Soma mystery must still be worked out.[5]  The tag verses of the Vasiṣṭha
hymns give the priest's personal point of view:
    O Agni, bring great riches to our patron... (7.1.24)
Geldner points out that Vasiṣṭha is the <u>Purohita</u> or house priest of the
prince <u>par excellence</u>.  Yet in the famous hymn to Indra based on the
battle of Sudas there is evidence of reward for devotion:
    200 cows, two wagons full of young girls - I who have
    rated this - circumambulate it                (7.18.22)
The ritual action of circumambulation of his own share of the spoils may
be a signal for the future power shift in which the priests come to be
the keeper of the cows.  In the hymns to Mitra-Varuna from Maṇḍala
Seven there is more priestly concern:
    The priest (<u>vipra</u>) directs his hymns (<u>brahmāni</u>) to you,
    O Mitra-Varuna, so that you may fill, as it were, all his
    autumns with your power (<u>kratu</u>)            (7.61.2)
There is a fear of death in the Vasiṣṭha hymns which is never voiced by
the warriors in the epic, but it appears that the death may also cult-
related and for that reason beyond human skill and cunning:
    This priestly task, of Gods Mitra-Varuna, has been made for
    you who get us across all difficult passages.
                                                  (7.61.7)
Nowhere is their a concern about warriors or kings except for booty. Yet
the imagery of the Indra hymns indicates the singers' knowledge of the
martial arts. The domain of the priest is the cult and his hymns:
    This hymn, O Varuna-Mitra, is offered like bright Soma juice
    to the Wind.  Favour our songs of praise, wake thought and
    spirit...                                     (7.65.5)
The verse shows the poet-priest in his milieu.  His domain is thought
and spirit.  When the cult died out the domain of thought and spirit had
the hymns themselves to work on, and the mystical philosophy of the
Upaniṣads grew up. The same process of speculating and commenting on the
epic songs went on with the complication that the epic songs contained
the actions and thoughts of warriors.  Hopkins notes:
    The Hindu moral teachers (for they were truly that, while
    being as a body unscrupulous of rewards) felt the necessity
    of expunging or excusing the sins of those heroes who had
    gradually become national models of royal and knightly
    honor.  I conceive it possible that these priests, after
    spending much labour to expound what a king ought to be,
    would have made every effort to cause those heroes  who
    had now become from success and glory of war popular types
    of perfect knights to appear in a light consonant with the
    moral principles that priestly ethics would inculcate.[6]
It is my contention that the priests only came to work out "moral principles" and "ethics" when they had gained power over the warriors.  Since
actions not thoughts are concerns of morality, then I contend that the
warriors had already fashioned the limits of morality, and it is the
priests' tampering with their code that can be traced in the layers of
the epic.

        There is a reference in the triṣṭubh core of the <u>Mahābhārata</u>
to a reprehensible act termed <u>mitradhruk</u>. Since the term occurs 13 times
in the triṣṭubh verses as a usable term in direct speech it is possible
to conclude, with the help of an Avestan corollary, that <u>mitradhruk</u>

involved a violation of a contract made between two warriors to insure
an alliance and back-up protection in battle. The fact that the tristubh
text survives  indicates the scrupulous care in transmission.  It does
not rule out the fact that whole passages and stories may have been
left out.  The tristubh verses give no clues to the singer since most of
the verses are dialogue.  There is a story framework of tristubh verses
in the first book of the epic which suggests that a messenger was the
narrative device used to convey the dialogue.  It is fairly evident that
the priests did not compose the oldest layer of the epic.

Another method of considering what priests do when they assume
control of heroic songs is to consider the creation of a <u>persona</u>. Arjuna
Pandava is the chief hero of the oldest layer of the epic.  He steals
brides one after the other, but Yudhisthira is the King of Dharma. The
notion of Yudhisthira as King of Dharma is a Brahmanic <u>persona</u>.  There
is evidence that he has been created as a deliberate embodiment of a
generous, stupid king.  At some point of Brahmanic take-over of the epic
the hero was replaced by his brother.  Arjuna Pandava is a Vedic warrior:
> The early tale artlessly relates how Arjuna, the defender
> of the faith, shoots Karna when the latter is helpless.  Did
> the old morality revolt at this?  I think not.  But the new
> morality comes that says 'no noble (Aryan) knight will fight
> except on equal terms.'  What then are the priests to do?
> They turn to God.  It was Vishnu who shouted to Arjuna 'strike
> him now,' and the great hero, questioning not the word of God,
> thought with great reluctance, shoots his helpless foe.  Here
> says the priest, is the truth of this story.  Certainly Arjuna
> killed Karna thus; but, you may not cite it for a precedent
> against our 'code of war,' since God inspired the act from
> occult reasons, and that takes the deed out of our sphere of
> judgment.[7]

It is the complicated task of the linguist to sort out the
texts so that a fair assessment of both priests and warriors can result.
From preliminary investigation it seems that warriors fashion their own
morality codes, and it is certain that the warriors devise the means to
punish the violations of the code they live by.  Family honor or disgrace,
protection of life or murder, possession of wives or adultery, possession
of goods or stealing, truth swearing or false witnessing-all are the ken
of the warrior class.  Thus when the worship of Brahmins is to result in
"kingdom, great good, fame, achievements and progeny" it appears that a
natural system has been inverted.  The power in the Soma cult may be an
answer.  When the warriors lose their power to the priests, then the
preaching of the priests on morality is a sure sign of confusion of basic
caste claims.  Such a confusion results in what Hopkins terms "the
descent of religion and the ascent of morality."  It is only one more
step to the construction of a God who is the supreme arbiter of morality.
Vishnu - or Yahweh - both supreme and unerring in their pronouncements
made through the mouths or hands of priests.

Notes

[1] Louis Renou, _Religions of Ancient India_ (Schœken Books; New York), p.48.  "It has been constantly asserted that India is obsessed with religion; it might be equally well maintained that India takes no cognizance of religion, at least as an independent phenomenon. Religion is not conceived as a duty, or as a problem facing every human being on reaching maturity.  It is a heritage and a tradition. The only word which expresses it is _dharma_, which in the Veda designated certain standards applying particularly  to the world of the gods.  The term includes not only religion but all the ethical, social and legal principles associated with religion, and which together with it constitute the real meaning of life for the Hindu."

[2] Pratap Chandra Roy, trans. _The Mahābhārata_ (Calcutta), p.324.

[3] E.W.Hopkins, _The Social and Military Position of the Ruling Caste in Ancient India_ (Varanasi), pp. 7-8.

[4] Cf. Albert B. Lord, _The Singer of Tales_ (Cambridge),introduction.

[5] R. Gordon Wasson, _Soma: the Divine Mushroom of Immortality_.

[6] Hopkins, _Ibid_.

[7] _Ibid_.

ZEN AS A VIPASSANĀ-TYPE DISCIPLINE

Winston L. King
Colorado State University

## I.  Zen Is to Mahayana As Vipassana Is to Theravada

This phrase is intended to indicate the comparable positions of the two meditational techniques, known as Zen and vipassanā, within their parent traditions. That comparability will be interpreted here as a similarity of general function and emphasis.  Zen and vipassanā will be presented as simplified techniques for achieving some degree of immediate enlightenment in contrast to the more elaborate or slower methods usual in the main tradition.

### A.  Vipassana and Theravada

We shall first observe the position of vipassanā within Theravada Buddhism. Vipassanā is usually translated as "insight," or, more elaborately "the intuitive light flashing forth and exposing the truth of the impermanency, misery, and impersonality of all corporeal and mental phenomena of existence."[1]

Traditionally what is called vipassanā has always been viewed as the <u>sine qua non</u> of the attainment of enlightenment usually practised in tandem with the likewise traditional yogic-style jhānic discipline.  All experiences, even those of jhānic trance, must be submitted to its mode of awareness in order to achieve enlightenment, or even to make significant progress on the path toward enlightenment; it stands in some tension with the yogic elements embodied in the jhānic-trance techniques even though these latter are viewed as central to the meditative practice both in the scriptures and in the main Theravada tradition.  However by the time Buddhaghosa was writing his <u>Path of Purification</u>, the classic manual of Theravada meditation, circa 500 A.D., a special and somewhat atypical class of meditators was somewhat grudgingly recognized as orthodox; namely, the "bare insight workers" or the "dry-visioned saints" as others have called them.  Now it is this mode of practice which bypasses the monk-oriented jhānic pattern, and can be largely separated from that pattern as an independent method, that is today known as the Vipassanā Method and has become quite popular in some Theravada countries among both laymen and monks.  Its emergence as a special and lay-oriented meditational technique is less than a hundred years old, Ledi Sayadaw (1846-1923), of Burma being one of its leading popularizers.

We need to ask how this special methodology is related to the tradition as a whole.  With respect to the orthodox establishment, which is heavily oriented toward a scriptural literalism, vipassanā remains doctrinally correct.  Indeed doctrinal innovation is the thought furthest from the mind of the vipassanā meditator; on the contrary he sees himself as fully implementing the spirit <u>and</u> the word of the Buddha as contained in the Pali Canon.  Yet since the main emphasis <u>is</u> upon practice, i.e., practice of meditation, there is somewhat the same tension here as there is between any experientially oriented group and the more institutionalized versions of religious orthodoxy.  The practical-intensive character of vipassanā practice, which seeks to go directly and rapidly toward enlightenment <u>here and now</u> in this very life, may seem pushy, "revivalistic," and perhaps presumptuous to the average Buddhist layman or monk.  Are the experiences claimed by vipassanites

genuine or merely ego trips?  Should one be hoping-claiming to become a Stream-
Enterer in this evil age?  Why are they in such a hurry?

A brief glance at the ordinary layman's and monk's ways to salvation
(Nirvana) will give point to this contrast.  Popular Buddhist piety, as might be
expected, is a matter of trying to follow the five precepts in daily life, attend-
ing (lunar) sabbath day discourses by the monks at pagodas, the observance of such
customs as naming-days and "confirmation" (shimbyu) ceremonies for the boys, gen-
erosity to monks and Buddhist causes, and observation of Buddhist holy days and
seasons such as the Buddha's birth-date, enlightenment date, Wesak (Buddhist "Lent")
and the like.  But enlightenment itself is far far off.

As for the monk, he is technically the one who has vowed to become a direct seeker after Nirvana and his mode of life--without worldly cares or responsi-
bilities--is specifically constructed to forward that search.  Yet the monkish mode
of Nirvana-seeking (through the long intensive meditation necessary to perfect
jhānic powers) is beyond the capacities and desires of most monks.  So in the end
the average monk became a dog in the manger as it were, unable-unwilling to arduously
pursue the meditational path himself but contemptuous of lay efforts to meditate.
And thus in part because of this stand-off situation, a few pioneering monks and
laymen within the relatively recent past began to emphasize vipassanā as an independent method, valuable because of its non-technical demands and rapidity of result.

Hence the appeal of vipassanā--whose level of meditative awareness calls
for none of the transic expertise of the monk's traditional jhānic discipline--is
obvious.  Further it can be applied not only during meditation itself but to the
acts and objects of daily life.  Thus it is truly open to layman as well as monk.
And, since vipassanā by definition goes to the Buddhist root of the matter directly,
in centering its attention upon the impermanent, impersonal, and painful character
of all existence, its concentrated use impliedly makes much faster progress toward
final enlightenment and Nirvana than any of the more traditional methods, either
lay or monastic--quite desirable in view of the hitherto "retarded" meditational
status of the layman.  Indeed the contemporary advocates of vipassanā strongly
urge its special fittingness for this modern age of lessened spiritual capacities,
increased tensions, and scarcity of time and opportunity for the more extensive
meditational practice envisaged by the "orthodox" tradition.

B.  Zen and Mahayana

Turning now to Zen and its relation to the parent Mahayana tradition we
observe that it too embodies a special methodological emphasis--the rapid-sudden
and definitive attainment of enlightenment by means of meditation.  The name "Zen"
itself bears witness to this fact.  It is a phoneticization of the Chinese Ch'an
which in turn was a phonetic version of the Sanskrit term Dhyāna (Pali Jhāna) or
"meditation," suggesting that its main, even exclusive purpose, is some sort of
meditation.  Thus Zen is distinctive in its central emphasis upon meditation as a
spiritual means, largely at the expense of other modes such as ritual, scholarly
learning, and mantric recitation.

There is one relational difference from the vipassanā case which should
be noted in passing.  Vipassanā is not a genuine sect but an emphasis or special
interest within Theravada, whereas Zen is both emphasis and sect, or perhaps better,
an emphasis become a set.  As such it has its own succession of patriarchs, i.e.,
transmitters of the "Buddha-Mind-Seal," its favorite scriptures and rituals, its
organizational quality and ethos, and its institutions, both cultural and physical.
At times it has been looked upon as radical and extreme, even heretical.

Its special qualitative emphasis is well set forth in the Four Principles erroneously attributed to Bodhidharma, the putative founder of Zen in
China:

A special transmission outside the scriptures;
No dependence on words and letters;
Direct pointing at the soul of man;
Seeing into one's nature and the attainment of Buddhahood.[2]

What is immediately evident in the first statement, of course, is its
attempt to cut through the maze of ritual practices and scholarly distinctions to
the core of Buddhism--enlightenment.  For even though the gospel of Mahayana uni-
formly preached the doctrine that "Samsāra is Nirvana" and embodied it in the
this-worldly activity of the Bodhisattva type of life, perhaps even because of
this philosophy, the sharply defined actuality of enlightenment and the expectation of it became indistinct and diffused.  As among Theravada laymen, so also the
hope of a better rebirth largely ruled the aspiration of Mahayana laymen and even
that of many monks.  Still further, in the process of "deifying" the Buddha and in
spinning out new and subtle metaphysical theories in its scriptures, Mahayana made
supposedly immanent Buddhahood so grandiose a goal that only by great learning and/or
elaborate rituals could it be achieved.  Thus there built up anew the desire to
find a simple, direct way back into the heart of Buddhism, namely enlightenment
itself.

Zen purports to do this as directly as possible.  Its methodology is precisely adapted to the goal of achieving enlightenment both rapidly and definitively.
It deliberately remains "outside" the scriptures even as it faithfully memorizes
some of them--in the sense of not letting scriptural literalism stand in the way of
spiritual development nor mistaking learning for the reality of enlightenment itself.  So far as Zen is concerned it is upon actual existential effort by the individual that enlightenment depends.  Enlightenment (satori) comes by using a
vigorous, incisive meditative method which is independent of any such incidental
factors as monk's or layman's status, or particular degree of formal knowledge.
This "learning by doing" is the only truly Buddhist life-pattern according to Zen,
and its resultant "knowledge" the only genuine knowledge.

That Zen stands well within the main Mahayana tradition, even though
"outside" the scriptures methodologically, is evidenced in the third and fourth
principles.  Indeed these principles are a sort of boiled-down essence of certain
great Mahayana scriptures themselves.[3]  Direct pointing at the "soul" of man--
perhaps better, his inherent Buddha-self nature--and experiencing this inner awareness of basic-true self nature as the essence of Buddhahood, i.e., enlightenment,
presupposes much of the foundational Mahayana teaching.  For only in the context of
some kind of Absolute Oneness--variously called the Void (śūnyatā), Suchness
(tathatā), the unconditioned Buddha nature (Dharmakāya), Cosmic Mind (Ālayavijñāna)
as opposed to individual mind, does it make sense to speak of seeing into one's
original nature as constituting the achievement of Buddhahood.  Zen's primary
difference from other Mahayana sects is the radical seriousness with which it takes
the general dictum that samsāra is Nirvana, right here and now, its emphasis upon
the sheer immediacy and availability of enlightening knowledge, and the simplicity
of its methodology.  In respect to this last:  As with vipassanā, so here too the
method of attainment is direct and uncomplicated, presupposing neither great learning[4] nor technical meditative skill.

II.  The Same and Different Goal--And the Way to It

But further problems of analysis remain because of the very different contexts of the two in terms of the presuppositions and doctrines of their respective supporting traditions.  Thus by definition the goals of Theravada and of Zen, as Buddhist, are identical:  enlightenment.  Originally this was defined as the attainment of Nirvana, i.e., total detachment and release from rebirth (samsāra).  But here the identity ends and the difficulties of interpretation begin.  For, as is well known, a basic point made early in the Mahayana development was the radical difference between Mahayana and Hinayana (Theravada) conceptions of Nirvana.  The Hinayana arhat's presumed enlightenment, i.e., attainment of "Nirvana," is at most only a minor way-station on the road to the full attainment of Buddhahood, now promised to him as his true destiny.  Indeed this is the main thrust of the names "Mahayana" and "Hinayana":  The Great, Universal, Absolute Enlightenment Way as opposed to the small, partial, relative, enlightenment way.  And besides this major difference the Zen version of enlightenment is a still further variant of the Mahayana theme, more radically "Mahayanist" than any of the other Mahayana versions in opening up the prospect of here-now satori for all.

The basic nature of the Theravada view of Nirvana (which we take here as roughly equivalent to that of Hinayana) is quite clear.  Nirvana is a "going out" from the round of perpetual rebirth (samsāra); it is a "blowing out" of the flame of craving for continued existence as a sentient being in individualized space-time forms.  The Buddha, the Master Arhat, was called Tathāgata, the "thus gone" (out) one.  The arhat, as an already (in actuality) "blown out" or "gone out" man, continues to live within his space-time body-mind form for the rest of his allotted days but very detachedly; for he is now fully aware (enlightened) of the true impermanent, unreal, and anguished nature of all space-time existence.  Upon physical death, as a fully gone out man, he will never return to samsāric embodiment.  Samsāra and Nirvana are polar opposites; samsāra so to speak, is of value only for the purpose of its dissolution by nirvanic attainment through enlightenment.

But Mahayana from the time of Nagarjuna onward has with one voice proclaimed that samsāra and Nirvana are identical.  To set them apart from each other as the to-be-escaped-from and the Escape is the very essence of ignorance or non-enlightenment, according to Mahayana.  And Zen can be said to have adopted the principle that samsāra is Nirvana in its most radical possible form.  All goodness, including Nirvana, is to be found in the immediate here-now of embodied existence.  There is no transcendent reality called Nirvana which is beyond this present life, either in time or the hierarchy of being, as a final haven from temporal succession.  Enlightenment is the realization that here-now is all; that this ordinary mind is the Buddha-mind; that one's present existence is the final goal of all effort.

This then is the context in which we must relate Zen and vipassanā to each other.  The problem is to discern clearly where we have sameness in difference, without denying or emasculating the differences in that sameness which we seek to establish here.  In order to supplement the general positional likeness considered in the first section with specifics of method and result, the following points will be taken up in turn:  (1) What is the problem to be solved, the existential situation to be remedied, by enlightenment, as perceived by Theravada-vipassanā and

Mahayana-Zen respectively?  (2) Are their respective techniques for achieving
enlightenment comparable?  (3) In what ways are the respective enlightenment experiences alike or different?

A.  The Problem to Be Solved By "Enlightenment"

As Buddhist, both Zen and vipassanā define the human problem to be
solved by enlightenment as two-fold:  The congenital human ignorance (as to the
true nature of reality), embodied in the ordinary human habits, feelings, and
knowledge with respect to space-time existence; attachment, intellectual and
emotional, to the products of this ignorant "knowledge."  All other undesirable
aspects of the human predicament flow from this double source.

But obviously, given the radically differing Mahayana and Theravada
views of that from which man is to be freed, and that to which he is to attain,
the respective meanings of both "ignorance" and "attachment" will be quite differ
ent.  We may, for example, observe the results of this difference quite con-
cretely and specifically in the traditions of the Buddha's own enlightenment experience.  It is described thus in the Pali Canon:

> When I knew thus, saw thus, my mind was freed from the canker of sense-
> pleasures and my mind was freed from the canker of becoming and my mind
> was freed from the canker of ignorance.  In freedom the knowledge came
> to be that I was freed, and I comprehended:  Destroyed is birth, brought
> to a close is the Brahma-faring, done is what was to be done, there is no
> more of being such and such.[5]

The basic meaning of this passage is clear:  Saṃsāra has been clearly
seen for what it is--an uneasy dream, or even nightmare, which is produced by greed,
hatred, and delusion, and which is intrinsically impermanent, unreal, and painfilled.  To "see things as they truly are" is to see through the false appearance
they present to the ordinary awareness--including that of an enduring, identical
selfhood--into the empty depths.  To know this existentially in personal experience
is to be freed from the ignorant attachment that produces rebirth; it is to become an "enlightened" or "gone out" man.

How then does Zen interpret the Buddha's (and all genuine) enlightenment?
A contemporary Zen roshi, Shibayama Zenkei, thus describes it:

> When Sakayamuni Buddha, the founder of Buddhism, saw the morning star
> glittering in the sky at dawn on the 8th of December, his long ascetic
> discipline came to an end, and his spiritual eye of Enlightenment was
> opened.  The sutra says that the first words uttered by Buddha on that
> occasion were:  "Wonderful, wonderful, wonderful indeed!  Every being on
> earth is without exception endowed with the wisdom and virtues of the
> Tathagata.  Only because of one's ignorance and attachments is one unable
> to come to this realization."[6]

Yes, this too is Buddhist enlightenment, but how differently conceived
from the Theravada understanding!  Herein the continental divide between Theravada
and Mahayana has been fully crossed.  Enlightenment does not free one from samsāra
but in and to samsāra.  Its saint is not the "gone out" arhat, but the "come in"
Bodhisattva.  While Theravada sees the Buddha's enlightenment as superior to yogic
attainment because it more completely cuts him off from and out of samsāra, Zen's

version sees it as superior because it more fully puts the Buddha (and all the enlightened) <u>into</u> some sort of <u>unity</u> with saṃsāra.

We must now ask the question: From what kind of ignorance then does
this Zen type of enlightenment deliver us? What is the significance of seeing
reality as it truly is in <u>this</u> manner? To take the last question first: It is obviously, as already noted, to see this present life itself as the locus of Nirvana.
It is to perceive the experienced cosmos as holy, to sanctify existence as such
in all its many forms, to glorify the sheer isness of life in this universe. The
universe is the manifold manifestation of the Absolute Buddha-Body (<u>Dharma-kāya</u>)--
which means that to <u>be</u>, is to be holy. The emptiness or void which <u>the</u> Zen Mahayanist sees in his enlightenment is not the single-valued zero of Theravada's <u>anattā</u>
nor even the negatively conceived Nirvana, but the empty-Fullness, the Full-because-
empty Śūnyatā--<u>void</u> of partializing characteristics, <u>full</u> of Absolute Reality. And
the ignorance <u>which</u> is overcome in Zen is the ignorance of our inherent oneness
with this absolute Buddha Nature. To assert the reality of our separateness from
this Buddha nature, even in our sin and finitude, is the essential ignorance. Indeed the sense of sin and finitude as separative from Buddha nature comprise that
ignorance.

The same kind of actual difference within sameness of terms applies to
"attachment" of course. In both Zen and vipassanā, attachment to unreal entities,
especially ordinary selfhood, is destroyed in enlightenment, cannot exist simul-
taneously with it. In Theravada the basic attachment is to one's own selfhood as
a real entity. Attachments to objects or persons outside oneself are but the
peripheral forms and fruits of <u>self</u>-attachment; destroy the core and its external-
ized forms will disappear. Thus by every conceivable means Theravada-vipassanā is
geared to destroy the central sense of integral selfhood which is the basic attachment.

But if in Mahayana-Zen, self-nature is also Buddha nature, and its par-
ticularistic isness is holy, what does "attachment" then signify? Logically derived from its conception of the true relation of individual to cosmos, attachment
here means attachment to the <u>limitations</u> of the self. It is attachment to the individual selfhood as <u>over against</u>, or <u>separate from</u>, the Ground of the cosmos, the
Dharma-kāya, or Śūnyatā; or attachment to beings, (my) being <u>versus</u> Being; attachment to conventional, acculturated mind as distinguished from universal-cosmic
Mind--in fact to <u>any</u> dualistic feeling or conception which separates "me" inwardly
from some "part" of myself or outwardly from the environing society and cosmic life.

Thus it is obvious that in both vipassanā and Zen enlightenment there is
a fundamental alteration--ideally the complete elimination--of the narrowly
individual-personal mode of consciousness. No longer is the "self," however conceived, to be experienced as an entity <u>apart</u> from the environing reality. In
vipassanā, enlightenment is the existential realization of the purely relative and
fragmentary nature of empirically understood and experienced individuality; the
"self" is placed squarely in the midst of the stream of cause-effect relationships
and reduced to a coagulation of impersonal elements--the result of "dependent
origination." The "self" as an entity is negated out of existence intellectually
and out of experience by a "selfless" awareness. In Zen the process and result are
conceived and experienced more positively, with individual mind become Universal
Mind, human nature become Buddha Nature, and the individual experiencing himself as

one with the flow of Life or Reality, even by means of his real-but-not-separate
selfhood.  Zen would interpret dependent origination as interdependent origination and interdependent mode of being.

But if the "negative" result of enlightenment in either mode is thus
somewhat the same--the destruction of the usual sense of selfhood--what of the
"positive" aspect of the new liberated-from-self consciousness?  Clearly, as noted,
one is an experience of freedom from space-time particulars and the other an experience of freedom within those particulars, even a new and more direct partici-
pation in and with them.  The Theravada model of achieved success is the detached
monkish arhat, and the Mahayana-Zen model is that of the Bodhissatva type individual.

That there is thus a basic qualitative difference here can scarcely be
denied by even the most ardent ecumenist.  It is the contrast flowing out of the
basic Theravada-Mahayana master models:  the world-withdrawn arhat and the world-
involved bodhisattva.  Their respective cultural and religious influence is profound.  And the modern vipassanā movement in Theravada may perhaps be interpreted
as a recognition of this, and to be a movement of a limited sort toward the
bodhisattva ideal.  For even though the avowed goal of vipassanā is the fastest
possible attainment of a world-denying Nirvana, its practice has now been fully
opened to laymen.  That is, even though it is Theravada dogma that an arhat mode
of life is impossible for one in the lay state, the stages up to that level are
possible to the layman.  He can fruitfully combine or relate vipassanā meditation
to his daily life.

B.  The Methods

As already suggested the vipassanic approach to enlightenment has neither
time for, nor basic interest in, the development of meditational (yogic or jhānic)
expertise, however traditional or helpful in an auxiliary way.  This latter indeed
may be an obstacle, either as giving a false sense of having arrived at the ultimate goal (Nirvana) or as being a subtle form of attachment to the self--in being
pleasantly attracted to one of its states.

But even more radically, of course, the whole jhānic effort may be by-
passed.  When this is done and vipassanā is begun directly, no attainment of the
deep transic states is even attempted.  What is called neighborhood or access
concentration is all that is required, which is but one step, so to speak, above
the ordinary level of attention.  It must be quite intense in its own way.  For
example, it is one-pointedly exclusive attention given to rise and fall of the ab-
domen in breathing, to the touch of the breath upon the nostril, or to a dominant
sensation; but it does not lock out all other sensory input with the absoluteness
of a hypnotic trance.  Thus as a method vipassanā is essentially quite simple, a
kind of meditation for which anyone has the requisite "equipment."

The "requisite equipment" for vipassanā is two-fold:  The perceptual experience of changingness within one's own body-mind (an existentially tangible
experience of impermanence, unreality, and pain):  and the mind's ability to detachedly observe such personal-internal change.  This latter may need development,
but as is the experience of change, it too is intrinsic to every human being.  The
vipassanā method then is essentially no more than the introspective-objective observation of one's own being.  Its main outlines are set forth succinctly in the
following canonical text:

A monk should dwell in body contemplating body (as transient), ardent, composed and mindful, by restraining the dejection in the world
that arises form coveting.  So with regard to feelings . . . to mind
. . . and to mind states.[7]

What is going on here is obvious:  One's _own_ "self," i.e., body-mind,
is being identified with the flux of natural processes in the environing world-
order, _without remainder_.  There are no loopholes, no escape hatches.  All that
"I" am is just that process--unless it be the power of detached attention.  (But
that does not constitute a separable entity in Theravada thought.)  And when this
type of self-attentiveness has been carried on assiduously for a length of time,
especially as applied even to the thoughts of the self-attended "I," the hold of
"self" upon mind and affection is broken.  There is no longer a "self" to be
attached to, nor a "self" to be attached.  Thus in a reductive way, the individual is no longer separate from the world about him either in thought or experience.

It might be put in other words thus:  The individual so conditioned becomes a self-aware, living embodiment of the Theravada view of individualized
existence as impermanent, unreal, and painful.  And he no longer needs to consciously force himself to think, "I am impermanent, unreal, painfilled process,"
but he is now aware of this in his very nerve fibers themselves, in his sub-
conscious emotions, and everyday mode of existence.  And in being thus aware, he
is freed from the hold of all pains and pleasures and finds himself--or _some_
self or other--at peace.

The Zen methodology has been so much written about that here it needs
only a brief sketching.  Just as with vipassanā--but with the hope of freedom
_into_ the world rather than _from_ it--Zen seeks to destroy that mode of awareness
which makes us experience ourselves as separate entities.  And it seeks, again
like vipassanā, to do this as directly and unambiguously as possible.  But in this
connection two somewhat divergent Zen modes must be noted.

Sōtō proposes to destroy the ignorant attachment which grows out of mis-
placed selfhood rather gently and gradually.  Following the lead of Dōgen who proclaimed that sitting in Zazen was _per se_ Buddhahood, or Buddhist activity--that is,
that nothing spectacular apart from what was thus and there experienced is to be
expected--Sōtō seeks the complete but not forced harmonization of breathing and
body-rhythms.  This breath and body harmony is to become so complete and deep-seated
that its organic unity permeates all that one does, till eventually (and perhaps
suddenly) any sense of separate self-hood is gone from anything and everything that
one does.

Now Rinzai, with its kōan technique, seeks to force the pace of the destruction of separative self-awareness.  The meditator is instructed to concentrate
intensely and strenuously upon his kōan--even repeating it mantrically sometimes.
Day and night, both sitting in meditation and in his other activities, it is never
absent from his attention.  He is continually trying to "solve" or "understand"
it.  References to its "meaning" or to statements in Buddhist tradition about it
are firmly, even harshly, rejected by the master.  This total concentration wears
down the critical or speculative mind, indeed is presumed to destroy even the
"conceptual mind" and leave the meditator in a benumbed, frustrated state called
the Great Doubt, in which the meditator can no longer feel or think about anything else _but_ the kōan; nor yet feel or think about it in any of his ordinary
"meaningful" ways.  His mind has been "killed" and his will exhausted.  But if

by some remnants of that "exhausted" will, or by some impulse of a new and different will-force, he is able to push on with the kōan effort and plunge into the abyss by letting go his frantic attempts to sustain the old-self style of meaning and importance, then after he "loses both body and mind,"

> "Brought to life again, suddenly one experiences a great joy like that of drinking water and knowing in his own self its coldness or its warmth.[8]

No longer is he a subject or spectator in a divided subject-object world, but integrally, spontaneously active in and with cosmos, one with the Buddha mind.

To return to the kōan methodology: Rinzai teachers assert that the kōan is the device par excellence for arousing or solidifying that doubt which in the end is one's salvation. Deliberately avoiding all intellectual complications and pushing the meditator on through to the end despite emotions pro and con, the kōan discipline produces crisis and breakthrough. It is viewed as a ruthlessly benevolent and efficient means to enlightenment. Thus Hakuin speaks sadly about a priest of the Eshin temple who took some forty years to achieve his enlightenment but who, if only he had had a good kōan to work on such as Mu or "three chin of flax,"

> "would most certainly have clearly realized that he himself was the body of Ultimate Reality. (And) this he would have done in one or two months or in a half a year at most. But in fact he must have used up the vitality of a full forty years by relying on the results and virtue of calling-extolling the Name and reading the scriptures.[9]

Despite all the mystique which has gathered about this method, especially with respect to the statements of the roshi to the meditator and the presumed necessity for his services in attaining Zen enlightenment,[10] the method remains, like vipassanā, _essentially_ simple and open to all.

There is no deepening transic consciousness aimed for in zazen--meditators keep their eyes open and are instructed not to try to achieve a blank no-thought ecstacy--nor is the enlightenment experience itself as we shall see later, a transic experience. The process is the simple but difficult one of breaking down those habitual thought, feeling, and action patterns in which thought and action, mind and body, inside world and outside world, oneself and Ultimate Reality (Buddha Nature) are separated from each other. And the kōan device in this sense is the simplest possible means for accomplishing this purpose.

To recapitulate: It seems reasonably clear from the preceding discussion that both Zen--particularly Rinzai--and vipassanā methods in general do seek to bypass the slower and more traditional methods of achieving enlightenment. And both do it, with due regard to their quite different doctrinal contexts, by a _function-ally_ similar method: single-minded destruction of a separative self-awareness. It may be further said that an even great degree of similarity of method may be found between kōan Zen and a quite recent development in vipassanā, namely the Sunlun method. Indeed one might say that Sunlun is to ordinary vipassanā what Rinzai is to Sōtō Zen--a maximum-intensity method devised to forcefully accelerate the pace toward enlightenment.

The Sunlun method is named after a local area in Burma in which an illiterate farmer (1878-1952), later called Sunlun-guchyaung Sayadaw (Sunlun-caves Teacher), discovered the rapid success of intensive meditation largely on his own.

According to his followers he became an arhat within a few years after beginning
his quest.  His method is largely devoid of any but the most basic Buddhist doctrinal statements--primarily that since saṃsāra so thoroughly embodies impermanence,
unreality, and pain it ought to be escaped as rapidly as possible.  It is popularly
known as "the rough-breathing method" and is a crash-course in meditation aimed at
so intensifying the meditator's awareness of the painfulness of individualized existence that he will rapidly break through into a fully existential no-self awareness.  In essence the method intensifies the awareness of the inherent painfulness
of embodied existence almost to the breaking point by rough, strong and continued
breathing.  The meditator relentlessly pushes on to the end in view with a kind of
frantic haste.  The following three maxims of the Sunlun Sayadaw will give us the
flavor of the method:

(1)  "The uncomfortable is the norm; the comfortable will set us adrift
     on the currents of saṃsāra."

(2)  "Do not rest when tired, scratch when itched, nor shift when cramped."

(3)  "Be rigorously mindful of the awareness of touch."[11]

The basic thrust of this methodology is clear:  It is an internalizing (at pressure cooker speed and intensity) of the Theravada conviction of the inherent emptiness and suffering of existence, making it so completely visceral that every breath
one draws, every physical sensation he experiences, bears out the truth of this view
to the diligent meditator without the nedessity of even _thinking_ about it.

Now, it is this "non-thinking" aspect which relates the method so closely
to the Zen Kōan method which, as we have seen, likewise aims specifically at cut-
ting off all conceptual _thought_ about the central issue of life-death (saṃsāra).
The specific Sunlun method which achieves conceptual cut-off, and thereby comes
closest to Zen, is contained in items two and three above.  Further and more specific directions forbid _any_ thinking-about, even to the extent allowed in the Ma-
hasi Sayadaw vipassanā method where one may think "itching, itching," or "hurting,
hurting" about his cramped limbs--and "if necessary" may scratch or stretch, thinking all the while "scratching, scratching" or "stretching, stretching."  Not only
is no such "necessity" envisaged by Sunlun, but even the mental note of "itching"
is forbidden.  The more the itching increases the more one concentrates his total
attention on the itching itself, filling his total awareness with the sensation.
Not even one sliver of thought must be allowed to intrude between the meditator's
full attention and the experience itself, or better, hide anything of the true
character of saṃsāra from full awareness.

The touch motif is also a significant one.  Primarily it applies to the
touch of breath on the nostril or upper lip; and as with incidental sensations such
as itching, which may need to be "attended to" by attention when they arise during
meditation, this primary focus of attention is never to be thought about, but only
felt.  And lest the attention wander in the slightest the heavy forced (rough)
breathing technique is suggested.[12]  In periods _in between_ meditation sessions, one
may keep alive something of this sense of direct touch with saṃsāra, so to speak,
by keeping himself consciously aware of the physical touch-sensation as he handles
the objects of his trade.  A contemporary Sunlun devotee, much in official life and
possibly with a somewhat more permissive enthusiasm for the technique than the Sayadaw, suggested to the author that this touch-awareness could be kept functioning
"even while holding a cocktail glass."

And finally, in a manner guaranteed to fully maximize the sheer sensation-
awareness of breathing, the breath is to be tightly held for a continuing period of

time after an initial 50 to 100 full strength inhalations and exhalations.  While
the breath is thus held "the whole body is watched internally."  Full attention is
to be given to the dominant, and usually painful, sensation wherever and whenever
it arises and, as with the breath earlier, concentrated without wavering or lapse,
face to face with it as though in combat, for as long as is physically and mentally
possible.  Then, in language remarkably like some descriptions of the Zen kōan concentration, it is said:

> When the mind has penetrated into the sensation the meditator will no longer
> feel the form of his foot, or arm or body; he will no longer feel that "I"
> am suffering.  These conceptual notions will be replaced by a simple, clear
> awareness of sensation alone.  With bated breath, tensed body, and forti-
> fied mind he should exert pressure against the pressure of the sensation un-
> til he is able to penetrate it, to dwell within it, watching it, without
> thinking any thought connected with it till finally the sensation is com-
> pletely consumed or ended.  It will be noticed that the important element
> in the technique is intentness.[13]

Mutatis mutandis we seem to have a Zen-like experience here.  Just as boring into the
kōan produces the "doubt mass"--the embodied essence of the Great Matter of life and
death with which one is in actuality struggling during meditation--so here there is
the "tangibilizing" of the whole matter of samsāra as impermanent, unreal, painful
in one "ball" of agonized resolution as one tries with all his might to keep his
attention viscerally in touch with the painfulness of self-being till it shall be
destroyed.  Such a method which first-personalizes the whole problem of existence
can lead to a crisis experience like Zen's Great Death.

A contemporary practicer of this method relates that several times she had
felt herself to be on the verge of a decisive breakthrough to a new order of awareness, but that the delusion of a "pool of ecstacy" into which she kept falling, and
the sheer wracking painfulness of keeping her full attention unwaveringly on the
mounting pain sensation itself, grew too great to bear.  Sometimes it seemed indeed
as though she were on the point of physical death:

> One day while I was practising at home I felt that my body was dashing away
> at a terrific speed towards something but I did not know what.  Like a run-
> away car crashing against a rocky hill I thought I would be smashed to pieces.
> A great fear seized me and I jerked myself away from that sensation.  I real-
> ized that I had missed a great experience.  I knew I should have faced that
> terrible sensation without fear.  With mindfulness as my only stay, I should
> abandon myself to whatever happened.[14]

After several such experiences, she came at last to realize what was involved:

> Only when I looked back I realised that I had instinctively turned back.
> The reason was quite simple:  I did not want to be free from what is
> Suffering; for the end of suffering meant the end of life . . . that is,
> the unending cycle of rebirth must be ended . . . .  I realised that my
> desire for life had made me turn back from the bound of freedom . . . .
> I saw that the road to Deliverance lay not in wallowing in the pool of
> ecstasy but in breaking through the blazing pathway of painful sensa-
> tions.[15]

In reading this one cannot but be struck with its great likeness to Hakuin's dramatic picture of the Zen meditator brought to the verge of despair in his struggling

with the koan--actually a struggle with his own self-identity--set forth in the imagery of a mountain climber:

> The steep face of the cliff, covered with slippery moss, offers no place
> for a foothold, he can neither advance nor go back. Only one thing re-
> mains: death. For support he has but an ivy plant, which he grasps with
> his left hand, and an arrowroot runner to which he clings with his right
> hand. And there for a time his life continues to hang (as) on a thread.
> Then if, of a sudden, he should let go with both hands there would be a
> dismembered body dashed to pieces, without so much as a dry bone remain-
> ing.[16]

And lastly there is a distinct parallel in the prescribed modes of achieving a breakthrough in Zen and Sunlun. In the former there is the intensive sesshin
of a week or more in which the meditator hopes to attain his initial satori. And
in Burma, U Win Pe, a contemporary Burmese Sunlun adherent, counsels an intensive
period of two weeks at a time, with continuous meditation periods up to 8 or 10
hours at a stretch, in order to break through to the state of "the knowledge of a-
rising and passing away" (uddayabbayānupassanā-ñāna) of all phenomena. It seems to
be roughly equivalent to the Stream Enterer stage--a definitive and permanent destruction of the self illusion, the first of four final stages in the attainment of
Nirvana--and perhaps comparable to a Zen first satori, as we shall note below.

Nor for that matter is this Sunlun rapidity of attainment by intense practice absolutely a novel emphasis in Theravada as a whole. We read the following in
the Pali Canon relative to setting up of the Four Stations of Mindfullness, i.e.,
meditative concentration on the body, feelings, thought, and ideas:

> "Or not to speak of one year bhikkhus, whoso shall thus practice these
> Four for six months . . . five months . . . four . . . three . . . two
> . . . one month . . . half a month only, in him one or two kinds of
> fruit may be looked for: either in this present life The Knowledge, or,
> if there be yet residuum for rebirth, the state of him who returns no
> more.[17]

Indeed the passage goes on to say that even _seven_ _days_ of such meditation may produce
the above result.

## C.  The Resultant Experiences

It remains to compare the _experiences_ growing out of the Zen and vipassanā
practices respectively, in particular Rinzai Zen and Sunlun vipassanā. And here in
its most crucial form we face the problem of difference in sameness and sameness in
difference, _both_ in the formal rather technical accounts of the two that are available to us, _and_ especially in the experiential quality which presumedly lies under-
neath the formal descriptions.

As to the formal descriptions we must return to the definitional statement of "enlightenment" as the crowning experience in each case. But we also must
now ask, in the light of the differing doctrinal-traditional backgrounds, what does
"enlightenment" represent by way of _experience?_ Still further we face the question
of _degree;_ for while each tradition holds forth the ideal of a final achievement of
full and complete enlightenment, each one also allows for an initial experience having genuine enlightenment quality but requiring further "maturing," "developing,"
or "deepening."

To take Zen first:  Whatever the "official" language, it is always taken
for granted that even the initial, instantaneous kenshō experience in Rinzai is
"qualitatively" but not yet "quantitatively" full enlightenment so to speak; or
that the "totality" of <u>enlightenment</u> is received, but the <u>person</u> is not "totally"
enlightened.  That mode of awareness which he has experienced in the first kenshō
must not be fully existentialized in his every thought, word, and action.  He has
had only a first glimpse of the true nature of enlightenment.  Sōtō also agrees:

> This is not to say that merely knowing one possesses the Buddha Nature
> is equivalent to being enlightened . . . .  One has to know of this
> possession, and still train, <u>in order to realize it to the full</u>.[18]

In any case nowadays the "post enlightenment" development of enlightened awareness
is usually taken for granted.

What is the case with vipassanā?  Given the difference in context, it is
essentially the same in this respect, except that in Theravada the process is for-
malized into four distinct stages:  Stream-enterer, Once-Returner, Non-Returner, and
Fully Enlightened One (arhat).  (These may occur in the same life, or in successive
ones.)  Now this enumeration by "stages" is often used by Zen writers to indicate
the distinctive difference between Theravada and Zen enlightenment, i.e., "gradual" as opposed to "sudden" enlightenment.  But in view of the long efforts to a-
chieve this breakthrough in Zen, its post-satori development which we have just noted, and the suddenness with which each of the four stages as well as the suddenness
with which enlightenment occurs in Theravada, the distinction seems hardly viable.[19]

As to this last:  Not only, as noted, may the seeking time be short, but
attainment is instantaneous.  (This latter facet of Theravada is perhaps unknown, or
only slightly known, to those in the Zen and Mahayana tradition.)  Thus, with respect to the attainment of arhatship (full enlightenment) Ānanda is portrayed as
having received it in a split second the night before the First Council after the
Buddha's death:

> " . . . having passed much of that night in mindfulness as to body, when
> the night was nearly spent thinking:  'I will lie down,' he inclined his
> body, but (before) his head had touched the mattress and while his feet
> were free from the ground--in that interval his mind was freed from the
> cankers with no residuum (for rebirth) remaining."[20]

Not only was the occurrence sudden (and there are many like instances recorded in
the <u>Path of Purification</u>), but there is besides an emphasis upon the breakthrough
<u>quality</u> of the new insight even at the first and lowest level experience level of
Stream Enterer--again in striking likeness to the Zen first satori.  Some Zennists
at least have been inclined to insist upon the dogma that Theravada "enlightenment" is a gradual clearing of inner vision, and Path attainment is only the final
focussing of insight, the maximizing of what was known before, hence not a fully
new breakthrough, as in Zen.  However Buddhaghosa calls the direct knowledge of
Nirvana that first comes to the Stream-Enterer a "change of lineage" in his type of
consciousness and describes it as follows:

> Change-of-lineage knowledge is like the man with eyes.  Nibbana is like
> the moon . . . .  Change-of-lineage knowledge's seeing the clear nibbana
> when the murk that concealed the truths has disappeared is like the man's
> seeing the clear moon in the sky free from cloud.[21]

It may be added that this Nirvana-awareness, is brand new at this stage.
And in continuing structural likeness to Zen, in which "big" and "little" satoris

are subsequently experienced, this direct Nirvanic awareness is repeatable with
practice and is also perceived afresh with the attainment of each of the succeed-
ing stages.

We must go on to repeat that the <u>interpretation</u> of this breakthrough experience of course varies with the Mahayana and Theravada contexts despite the just-
noted similarities. For Mahayana-Zen it means breaking down all dualisms of experience and thought in a positive way: one sees his original Nature; knows himself
as a Buddha, or finds that Buddha-nature is indeed his own nature, identical with
his "ordinary" self; that his individual wave-mind is one with the cosmic ocean-
mind, and the like. Theravada-vipassanā interprets <u>its</u> enlightenment as "negatively" breaking down all dualisms, except perhaps that of saṃsāra-Nirvana; the self,
as different from the samsaric-elements that constitute it, does not exist; the self
<u>is</u> saṃsāra. But in the very knowing of this, the ultimately Real (Nirvana) is also
experienced by some power within the illusory self.[22] Self-as-saṃsāra and Nirvana-
as real are two sides of the same experiential coin.

The question then is: In what ways do these differing interpretations
affect the resultant experiences? First we may observe that there is in both satori
and Stream-Enterer attainment a fleeting but vivid and determinative sense of the
Unconditioned with-out any intermixture of self-awareness. D. T. Suzuki thus states
it for Zen:

> We now say that the "<u>Mu</u>!" and the "I" and the Cosmic Unconscious--the
> three are one and the one is three . . . which I call "consciously un-
> conscious" or "unconsciously conscious."

> But this is not yet a <u>satori</u> experience. We may regard it as corres-
> ponding to what is known as <u>samadhi</u> . . . . For Zen this is not enough;
> there must be a certain awakening which breaks up the equilibrium and
> brings one back to the relative level of consciousness, when a <u>satori</u>
> takes place . . . . Once this level is touched, one's ordinary con-
> sciousness becomes infused with the tidings of the unconscious.[23]

What occurs here is <u>first</u> a momentary sense of oneness in which all self-awareness
and all attendant distinctions (inner-outer, I-thou, subject-object) are blotted
out,[24] and <u>second</u> a return to ordinary consciousness, but a consciousness "infused
with the tidings of the unconscious," i.e., with a pervasive sense of unity, at-one-
ness with oneself and impliedly with the rest of reality at its deepest level.

This same enlightenment sense of unity-with-cosmos is more overtly but
<u>quite</u> characteristically expressed in the following passage:

> "Go deeper," the roshi said. "Question 'What is this Mu?'
> to the very bottom."
> Deeper and deeper I went . . . .
> My hold was torn loose and I went spinning . . . .
> To the center of the earth!
> To the center of the cosmos!
> To the <u>Center</u>.
> I was <u>There</u> . . . .
> The world no longer rides heavily on my back.
> It is under my belt."[25]

What is there comparable to this in Theravada sources?  Experiential statements like
the above are harder to come by; for in Theravada most of them are technically and
dogmatically phrased, so that even in experiential statements the special Theravada
doctrinal flavor is present.  Yet that in itself is significant, for the experiences
here recorded <u>are experienced in those terms</u>.

In some of the early scriptures, Theragāthā and Therīgathā (<u>Psalms of the
Brethren, Psalms of the Sisters</u>), we do sometimes find overtones of strongly positive emotional quality.  Thus:

> Buoyant in sooth my body, every pulse
> Throbbing in wondrous bliss and ecstasy.
> Even as cotton-down blown on the breeze,
> So floats and hovers this my body light.  (B 104[26])

But more characteristic is the more sober mood of the two following selections which
include in their statement the all important reasons for such "joy" as they do feel:

> To free my path from all that breedeth Ill
> I strove with passionate ardour, and I won!
> Craving is dead, and the Lord's will is done.
> Today is now the seventh day since first
> Was withered up that ancient Thirst.  (S 41)

> With thought of death I dally not, nor yet
> Delight in living.  I await the hour
> With mind discerning and with heedfulness.  (B 196[27])

Buddhaghosa, the scholastic philosopher of Theravada meditation, sometimes becomes
lyrical (for him) in describing the result of Path experience, ensuing upon the
attainment of direct Nirvana awareness.  Thus:

> As the Path comes into being it pierces and explodes the mass of greed,
> the mass of hate, and the mass of delusion never pierced and exploded
> before . . . .  It closes all doors to the states of loss.  It allays all
> enmity and fear.  It leads to the state of the Full Enlightened One's
> breastborn son.[28]

Obviously even this statement does not escape the rigorous doctrinal framework of
Theravada.

And finally there is the canonical description of the state of one who has
attained to Nirvana in this life, the arhat:

> Just as a rock of one solid mass remains unshaken by the wind, even so
> neither visible forms, nor sounds, nor odours, nor tastes, nor bodily
> impressions, neither the desired nor undesired, can cause such an one to
> waver.  Steadfast is his mind, gained is deliverance.[29]

These statements, of course come from the classical and traditionalized
experiences of arhats who are "gone-out" persons even in this life, and may not apply so directly to the lower orders of Stream-Enterer and Once-Returner nor to the
somewhat more emotional popularized and laicized versions of meditation carried on
by laymen (and even monks) today.  Nonetheless the detached life which neither dallies with thought of death nor delights in living, and when it does rejoice, rejoices
in its freedom <u>from</u> saṃsāra, remains the <u>ideal</u> life-style, the perfect model, for

all orthodox Theravada meditators, layman or monk, particularly for those in the intensive Sunlun practice. Its total emotional quality and life-consequences, therefore, cannot but differ essentially at this point from the Zen enlightenment freedom _for_ and _in_ saṃsāra as has been previously suggested.

Illustrative of this, the two following contemporary quotations speak for themselves. The first is from the Ledi Sayadaw, the teacher who did more than any other to spread the present practice of vipassanā among Burmese Buddhists:

> If the pleasure and joy experienced in vipassanā sukha, which is complete with the seven characteristics of sambodhi, be divided into 256 parts, one part of that joy and pleasure exceeds the worldly joys and pleasures of kings among humans, devas and Brahmas, so great is the joy and pleasure inherent in the sambodhis. "The flavor of the _dhamma_ exceeds all other flavors."[30]

The second is the account of the climactic experience of the vipassanā meditator whose death-awareness experience was noted above:

> One night I lay in a restful trance practising mindfulness of the bodily sensations. At first the sensations were not unpleasant as my body was throbbing softly. Later my whole body began to vibrate as if an electric shock was running through me. I no longer could be restful. I had to rally all my strength to be mindful of the sensations. The vibrations grew more and more violent. I went on being mindful unswervingly. My mindfulness was strong but the violence of the sensations seemed to match and challenge it. Mindfulness and sensations met in a death struggle in which fear caused by the thought, "What shall become of me?" had no place. When two things, namely the sensation and mindfulness existed, there was no place for I. The illusion of I was broken. As the sensations increased in violence the power of mindfulness matched its fearful intensity. I did not know how long this went on. Then suddenly like nerves bursting under a great strain there was a big explosion. The next thing I knew I was sitting crosslegs, my whole body wide open like the boundless sky, with nothing to hang on, nothing to cling to. It was an indescribable moment.
>
> I faced the dawn of the day paying my respects down at the household shrine with the simple prayer,
>
> > I take refuge in the Buddha
> > I take refuge in His Law
> > I take refuge in His Order of the Yellow Robe.

How many times all through my life had I uttered this prayer! But this time I meant every word of it. I knew I was crowned again with the Three Gems. There was nothing but peace in my heart.[31]

ENDNOTES

[1] _Buddhist Dictionary_, Nyanatiloka (Colombo:  Frewin and Company, 1956), p. 177.

[2] _Zen Buddhism_, D. T. Suzuki (New York:  Doubleday, 1956), p. 61.

[3] Such as the _Prajñāparamitā_, the _Avatamsaka_, and the _Lankāvatāra_ Sutras, for example.

[4] Thus, Hui Neng the Sixth Zen patriarch is traditionally said to have been illiterate.

[5] _Middle Length Sayings_ (I.249), Pali Text Society edition, I. B. Horner, tr.,(London:  Luzac, 1954), p. 303.

[6] _A Flower does not Talk_, Abbot Zenkei Shibayama, (Rutland:  Charles E. Tuttle, 1970), p. 161.

[7] _The Book of the Kindred Sayings_, F. L. Woodward, tr. (London:  Luzac, 1965), Volume V, p. 147 (Text:  V, 166).

[8] "The Fourth Letter of Hakuin's _Orategama_," tr. Winston and Jocelyn King and Tokiwa Gishin, _The Eastern Buddhist_ New Series (Otani University, Kyoto), V, No. 1, p. 98.

[9] _Ibid._, p. 111.

[10] But see _An Experience of Enlightenment_, Flora Courtois, Zen Center of Los Angeles, 1971, for the account of an "authentic" kenshō experience gained by an American woman without the guidance of a roshi.

[11] _The Yogi and Vipassanā_, Sunlun Shin Vinaya, (Rangoon:  Sunlun Buddhist Meditation Center), n.d., p. 14.

[12] In visiting a Sunlun type meditation center near Rangoon the author observed a room full of meditators practising rough breathing in time with a tape-recorded loud and sterterous version of the practice.

[13] _The Yogi and Vipassanā,_ pp. 28, 31.

[14] "A Buddhist Pilgrim's Progress," Daw Khin Myo Chit, _The Guardian_ (Rangoon:  February, 1963), p. 17.

[15] _Ibid._, p. 16.

[16] "The Fourth Letter from Hakuin's _Orategama_," p. 98.

[17] _Dialogues of the Buddha_, T. W. and C. A. F. Rhys-Davids (London:  Luzac, 1966), Part II, Suttanta XXII, 22 (D.ii, 314), p. 346.

[18] _Selling Water by the River_, Jiyu Kennett, (New York:  Random House, 1972), p. 55.  Italics added.

[19]See author's "A Comparison of Zen and Theravada Meditational Methods and Goals" in History of Religions, IX, 4, pp. 305, 315 for a fuller discussion.

[20]Book of Discipline, I. B. Horner, tr. (London:  Luzac, 1963), Book V, XI, 6(285), p. 396.

[21]Path of Purification, Nyanamoli, tr. (Colombo:  A. Semage, 1964), XXII, 10  p. 787.

[22]While the Sunlun material available to me does not specifically equate the "knowledge of arising and passing away" of all things, including the self, with the Stream-Enterer stage (when Nirvana is first seen), it is so much of the same essence that I am here equating the two for practical purposes.

[23]Zen Buddhism and Psychoanalysis, Fromm, Suzuki, and DeMartino (New York: Harper and Brothers, 1960), pp. 46-7.

[24]See also Three Pillars of Zen, Philip Kapleau (Tokyo:  Weatherhill, 1964), pp. 228.

[25]Ibid., pp. 253-4.

[26]From Psalms of the Sisters (S) and Psalms of the Brethren (B), Volumes I and II of Psalms of the Early Buddhists, tr. C.A.F. Rhys-Davids (London:  Luzac, 1932, 1937).  References are to stanza numbers.

[27]Ibid.

[28]Path of Purification, XXII, p. 14.

[29]Buddhist Dictionary, p. 99.

[30]Manuals of Buddhism, Ledi Sayadaw (Rangoon:  Union of Burma Sasana Council, 1965), p. 203.

[31]"A Buddhist Pilgrim's Progress," p. 19.